WALKING IN LIGHT

KELVIN CRUICKSHANK

PENGUIN BOOKS

PENGUIN BOOKS

Published by the Penguin Group
Penguin Group (NZ), 67 Apollo Drive, Rosedale,
North Shore 0632, New Zealand (a division of Pearson New Zealand Ltd)
Penguin Group (USA) Inc., 375 Hudson Street,
New York, New York 10014, USA
Penguin Group (Canada), 90 Eglinton Avenue East, Suite 700, Toronto,
Ontario, M4P 2Y3, Canada (a division of Pearson Penguin Canada Inc.)
Penguin Books Ltd, 80 Strand, London, WC2R 0RL, England
Penguin Ireland, 25 St Stephen's Green,
Dublin 2, Ireland (a division of Penguin Books Ltd)
Penguin Group (Australia), 250 Camberwell Road, Camberwell,
Victoria 3124, Australia (a division of Pearson Australia Group Pty Ltd)
Penguin Books India Pvt Ltd, 11, Community Centre,
Panchsheel Park, New Delhi – 110 017, India
Penguin Books (South Africa) (Pty) Ltd, 24 Sturdee Avenue,
Rosebank, Johannesburg 2196, South Africa

Penguin Books Ltd, Registered Offices: 80 Strand, London, WC2R 0RL, England

First published by Penguin Group (NZ) 2009
3 5 7 9 10 8 6 4 2

Copyright © Kelvin Cruickshank 2009

The right of Margie Thomson to be identified as the author of this work in terms of
section 96 of the Copyright Act 1994 is hereby asserted.

Designed by Mary Egan
Typeset by Pindar (NZ)
Prepress by Image Centre Ltd
Printed in Australia by McPherson's Printing Group

ISBN 978 0 14 301171 2

A catalogue record for this book is available
from the National Library of New Zealand.

www.penguin.co.nz

Some names in this book have been changed to protect privacy.

CONTENTS

INTRODUCTION

Spirit

'WHITE feather, white feather.' The spirit voice was coming through strongly and insistently. I was getting towards the end of a show in Brisbane. It was late, we'd already spoken to about 30 people, and Tracy, my agent, was giving me the look that says, 'It's time to go home', when a spirit voice began repeating 'white feather, white feather'. I asked the audience, 'Who knows anything about a white feather? Do you know what that means? That's what I'm hearing: white feather, white feather.'

Nobody responded. I kept asking though because the voice was now yelling at me, 'White feather, white feather'. Suddenly Tracy, who was at the back of the hall, saw a woman sitting tucked away in one of the rows, holding a white feather on her lap. She wasn't going to own up, too shy, but Tracy thrust the microphone at her and said, 'Kelvin, over here.'

The woman stood up and said, 'I've got a white feather.'

A woman then appeared in spirit and said, 'It's okay, it's not her fault.' I relayed this, and the poor woman in the audience broke down. It turned out that she'd witnessed her best friend being murdered by her boyfriend, and had carried a terrible burden of guilt ever since. She said in front of the audience, 'I'm so happy that you've said that because I've carried this burden because I couldn't stop him.' And the girlfriend in spirit just said, 'It's not your fault.'

The woman in the audience had brought the white feather as a symbol that her dead friend was an angel – her 'angel friend'. That's what led to the connection.

Almost every day I experience stories like this one. So far my life has been an incredible journey, but I can honestly say that I feel blessed to be able to help people experience the peace and joy that comes through the white light of the spirit world.

I am blessed to walk in the white light – the unconditional love of the angels, of Jesus, God, the Creator, the Universe – whatever expression you prefer. In this light we keep honest and true, and are at peace with ourselves and everything in life. We might stuff up – we all do – but we pick ourselves up and keep going. I tell people, 'Trust unto the light and be brave. It is through experience that we learn.' I believe the white light is my saviour and I will honour it until I cross into it; until I return home to the angels forever.

I am also blessed by my guardian angels, and spirit guides, who help me in every possible way. Margaret is my beautiful guardian angel who appeared to me, surrounded by an incredible white light, when I was about to end it all, and reminded me of why I needed to keep on living. She helps me through readings to do with children passing, and holds my hand as I see what I need to see. She helps me keep my head together. She loves me unconditionally, and I her.

Jesus himself has guided and supported me through my entire life. And my mother's father, Pop, or Monty, has been with me in spirit since I was eight years old.

Another great spirit friend first began to visit me when I started working on the television programme *Sensing Murder*. She was a white-haired old lady, very kind and very helpful to me, but I didn't know who she was. I mentioned this to one of the programme's producers, who emailed me a digital image of a white-haired old lady – the very same woman who had been appearing to me. It was Doris Stokes, the world's foremost psychic medium of the twentieth century, who worked in England up until her passing in 1987. Since then, Doris has continued to be a great friend to me. She helps me through the harder reads and is always very supportive. Doris loves live stage work and is present much of the time. She particularly comes through for people who have read her books. She'll say, 'That man in the crowd has read my book. Tell him I've met his dad and his brother Frank and they are together…' She hits the mark every time!

I have always seen, heard and felt spirit, but in my early years I had no idea what it all meant. It was just one freaky or scary thing after another.

But when I was 27 I had a breakdown and the things I'd been running away from all my life were suddenly laid out in front of me – they couldn't be ignored any longer. Spirit said, 'Wake up, Kelvin!'

For years I'd been losing myself in endless hard work, never stopping. When I did stop, that was when I finally confronted who I really was, and faced the reality of the gift that I'd been given.

That moment enabled me to look back over my life and finally see it for what it was. After the breakdown, I sat quietly with myself for the first time and acknowledged all the things from childhood that caused people to think I was crackers: the times I foresaw what was going to happen; the ghosts that I could see and talk to. Everything started to make sense, and I realised that this is the way I am. Everything finally fit together into the story you're about to read.

Since acknowledging and accepting my gift eleven years ago, life has changed in so many ways, most of them good. I'm grateful every day to the spirits that guide me and show me the way and allow me to help people, which is my goal in life. I never forget that without the white light and spirit, I'm just a guy who can cook. Nothing more.

CHAPTER ONE

The spirits of the land

I'VE SEEN spirit all my life. Even as a toddler in the early 1970s, living in a small house in a small New Zealand country town, Ngaruawahia, I always had 'imaginary' friends – people I could see that no one else could – and when I met people I always used to sense other people with them. Back then, it wasn't scary or strange. I just thought it was quite normal. I didn't know that it wasn't like this for everyone.

Ngaruawahia is one of those tiny little towns most people whizz through on their way to the cities of Auckland or Hamilton. You might stop for a pie, or twist your neck as you cross the bridge over the Waikato River to get a glimpse of the Maori King's Turangawaewae Marae. It's in heartland Waikato: surrounded by farms, both dairy and sheep, and some of the most beautiful, gently rolling countryside you can imagine. For us in the early 1970s, it felt like the centre of the world. It always seemed incredibly peaceful, although, as you'll see, it has a very bloody history that still resonates in the present for those, like me, who are sensitive to the spirit of people and land.

Dad – Les, or Crooky as everyone still knows him – was the hydatids control officer for the Raglan County Council, as it was known then. He still lives in Ngaruawahia and although he's retired he works part time at the dog pound. He has a special gift for animals – even really savage dogs just turn really soft and quiet around him. We call him the dog whisperer.

Mum – Heather – stayed at home with my older brother Murray and me for the first few years. She had formerly worked as a volunteer driver for the bus carrying handicapped children. I can remember going on the bus with her before I started school. That was an interesting eye-opener for me – I used to make those kids laugh! And from an early age I learned not to judge others. Mum went on to train as a teacher, and is now a reverend in the Anglican church – a very spiritual lady.

The person I loved most in the world was my Pop, my mum's father, Monty Haack. His wife Hazel, my Nan, I was also extremely close to. They lived in Ngaruawahia, about a kilometre down the road from our house. Once, when I was two or three, I ran away – all the way down the road, across several streets, just to get to Pop and Nan's house. Poor Mum was frantic, not knowing where I'd got to. But I was determined, and I always wanted to be with my Pop. He and I got on like a house on fire. He was a hard man who'd ruled his own family with a strong arm, but he was wonderful to me. I was his shadow, totally his shadow, and felt he understood me.

Before I was born he had a fish and chip shop on the main street of Ngaruawahia. He made my mother leave school when she was 13 so that she could work in the shop. He was one of those people who thought that girls didn't need an education.

Mum eventually proved him wrong however, returning to study to be a teacher at Waikato University when I was about seven.

Now she's more educated than many people.

By the time I was born, Pop was running an army surplus supply store. He was also a jack of all trades who could build or fix anything – in his spare time he'd be under a car or in the vegetable garden. He could make his own sinkers and tie his own flies for trout fishing. When whitebait season came around we'd be off to Tuakau with his tent and dogs. Parked on the side of the road, we'd catch the whitebait and Mum and Dad would come out to get it and sell it on the roadside for a few dollars.

Or we'd go out in his boat, netting fish. He had a massive smoker, double the size of a typical garden shed, where we'd smoke kahawai and mullet. We used to have the nets strung up and down the section and we'd mend the nets. To me, that was fun.

I was very easily bored and needed to be busy all the time. I'm still like that – I'm here to live, not to eat my lunch. As a youngster I was always looking for adventures and challenges, and Pop understood that. We'd get a load of coal and shovel it off the trailer into the coal shed, and then we'd go back to the mine and get another load ... he and I could do that all day. He'd tell me to dig up the garden with a shovel, or mow the lawns. I could chop kindling all day, making piles and piles of it. I used to love growing the veges.

Pop used to take me out to the garden at midnight – 'come on boy, get up' – when the worms would come to the surface. They were massive, a foot long, and we'd get out there with a torch and take a shovel load. You had to be real quick. The next day we'd go trout fishing. We used to do heaps of fun things like that.

When I was about four, Dad was promoted by the Raglan County Council to the post of hydatids control officer for the Rotongaro district, and our family left Ngaruawahia to live there. Rotongaro's not far from Ngaruawahia – about 20 kilometres out of Huntly towards the west coast. It was a tiny community, very picturesque and rural. Nearby was Waikowhai, a big coalmining community, and a few other rural villages – Glen Murray, Glen Alton, Glen Massey.

We lived in a small council house, one of three in a row on a hillside, and there was a wee petrol station down the road that only had petrol, no lollies!

Behind the house, we looked down over the rolling paddocks and from my bedroom window I could clearly see a stand of old, native bush that for some reason hadn't been cleared when the land was taken up for farming. Dad told me, 'You're not to go into that bush. It's too dangerous.' I think there was a well in there, or something that he was worried about. But from my point of view, all I wanted to do was go and play in the scrub.

So one day – I must have been about four – I ventured across the paddock and walked the fence line around the bush. It felt as though 100 eyes were looking at me – I could sense other people in this clump of scrub, watching me. I told myself I was only afraid because Dad had talked me into thinking the bush was unsafe. But after that, things were never the same again.

After I had paid that visit, spirit people came out of the bush and stood outside my bedroom window, which faced it, every night except at full moon. They were tupuna, the Maori ancestors, and they had their turkey feathers, tattoos, taiahas (long clubs) and patus (short clubs) and they'd be speaking to me in Maori.

The history of the land, which of course I knew nothing about at the time, was one of bloodshed and massacre. In the early nineteenth century, Te Rauparaha, a chief of Ngati Toa from the neighbouring Kawhia district, had been engaged in continual warfare with the Waikato tribes in the exact area where we were now living. We were pretty much living on a killing field, and the people I saw outside my window were, I now believe, victims of that warfare.

But as a four-year-old I was understandably very, very scared of them. I was too small to have any understanding of what they were and all I knew was that outside my bedroom, every night, were these terrifying people talking to me in Maori. I thought they were threatening me. So every afternoon, before the sun went down, I'd pull down the blinds over my window to prevent me seeing these people.

Dad would get really cross. 'What the bloody hell are these blinds down for?' And he'd pull them up. By the time I was ready for bed, I'd get to my room and flick the lights on and the roller blinds would be up and there'd be these people standing at the window!

This went on for about four years and is a huge feature of that part of my childhood.

IT WAS my Pop's death when I was eight that was to bring to an end the visitations by the Maori ancestors.

For me, his death was a terrible time, yet he's never really left my side and is the most consistent spirit presence in my life.

I remember vividly when it happened. I was staying in the spare room at Nan and Pop's place, sleeping in their old spring bed, being looked after by a friend of Mum's as all the adults were at the hospital with Pop. At about two in the morning I suddenly sat bolt upright in bed. Pop was standing beside me and said, 'Hey son, wake up.' I said, 'Hey Pop. What are you doing here?' He replied, 'I'm going away, but I want you to know that I'm always going to be there for you. I'm going to heaven, but you need to know that I'm always going to be there, and I'll come back whenever you need me and sometimes I'll just surprise you!'

'What's happened to you?' I asked.

'I've died,' he said. And I said, 'But I can see you!' I was sobbing by then – I was only eight after all.

He said, 'I know son, I've always known you can see.' He then gave me a big hug and left, just disappeared. The next thing I remember is standing in the hallway that ran straight through the house a couple of hours later. I heard the car come into the drive, and all the adults piled into the house – Mum, Dad, Nan and my mum's brothers John, Kev and Barry. And you could see it on their faces, really sad. Uncle Kev picked me up. 'You all right, boy?' he asked. I said, 'Pop has gone away.' They were trying to protect me, so they told me he was in hospital and was getting better, but I knew, and I told them, 'He told me he'd died.'

They put me back to bed and the next day Nan sat me on her lap out in the garden on Pop's swing, and said, 'I've got something to tell you.'

'Nan,' I said, 'I already know.' I told her what had happened. And she confirmed that he'd passed away during the night, just after 2 a.m. That's life, but to me it was devastating. It was really tough. I didn't want to talk for ages. I wasn't angry – I just missed him. Thirty years on I still do, although he's still around and I can talk to him any time I want. I have a strong sense of him when I'm out fishing, and often he'll come in before one of my big shows, or when I'm working on a murder case. I feel very supported by him.

He was much respected by local Maori, and after his death we were invited to scatter his ashes in Lake Tarawera, near Rotorua. That was a great honour, an incredible mark of respect from the Te Arawa people of that area. Lake Tarawera is a sacred place of great power and mythical significance to the Maori people – as I came to realise to my peril at a later stage of my own spiritual development.

We had a family service on the launch MV *Tarawera*, with Captain Jock, an old family friend who used to take cruises across the lake. We all took Pop's ashes and had to let them go into the lake, and I remember standing on the back of the launch with a handful of my Pop, not wanting to let go. I looked down into the lake's dark water and to my amazement could see his face smiling at me. He was whispering to me to let go, that he would be okay, and reminded me that I could see him any time I needed to. And with that, I let go.

Interestingly 30 years later Nan did the same thing when she passed over. Early in 2008 I was visiting Whangaroa, a stunningly beautiful harbour near the top of the North Island, which is world famous as a place to catch marlin. Thanks to Pop, I still love my fishing more than almost anything else! I was getting away from everything, at a beach where I couldn't get reception on my phone. Again, I was asleep in bed when I suddenly woke and sat bolt upright to find Nan and Pop standing there, together.

'What are you doing here?' I asked. And Nan said, 'Oh, I've just passed away, son! I've finally caught up with my love and I'm here with him.'

Sure enough, there they both were, looking young and happy. When you go into spirit you can be anything you want to be, whatever tickles your fancy. My Nan didn't like getting old, she thought it was a stupid idea, and she was always a very young soul. So when they came through together they were in their 30s, when they were at their happiest together. Nan was standing there looking gorgeous, and she said, 'But you need to check your phone.'

I was crying and sobbing, 'Oh Nan!' My uncle had passed a year or so earlier and he was there as well, it was a family reunion in spirit. I got in the car and drove about 15–20 kilometres into the hills away from the beach so that I could get some reception, and there were lots of messages saying Nan had passed – but of course by that time I already knew.

Nan, like Pop, had understood me more than anyone and had been an important figure all my life.

After Pop had died, she and Uncle Kev took over his role. We'd go tiki-touring everywhere, the three of us – whitebaiting, collecting cockles at Raglan and having a fire and feed on the beach, or playing in the mudflats to try and catch flounder. It was always neat with Nan and Uncle Kev, but never the same without my Pop.

Mum's side of the family love their hunting and fishing – if you want some meat, better go out and kill it yourself. I quite like that kind of living and still go down to hunt with them.

Uncle Kev was like a Dad to us. He's a cool dude who's remained a bachelor to this day with no kids, and after Pop died he was trying to make us a little bit happier.

On one occasion he decided we'd go on holiday, camping in the Coromandel. Kev had a Holden ute, called Dolly, so he slung a crate on the back – something to sleep in – that my brother and I got to paint. So we painted it inside and out, to match the colour of the ute.

You can just picture us: Dolly the ute with her name handwritten on by Kev, with a huge CV aerial about five times the length of the car, a few flags on it, bull bars, and the old visor to stop the sun coming in, complete with holes! We all thought he was a complete dag.

Because we were going camping we decided to take the dinghy. Now, the dinghy was being towed on a trailer, and had also been christened – Kev had handwritten 'Ugly-but-rows-well' along the side. We thought that was a hell of a hoot.

And, in true Kiwi fashion, we had an old canvas tent – pole in the middle and no ground sheet. It was the usual, 'We'll be right' attitude.

My brother and I were supposed to sleep in the ute, so we jumped in, all excited because we'd made mattresses in there and it was really cool. But the paint fumes were just horrendous, absolutely horrific, so we didn't last too long and all slept on the ground, in the tent.

Next morning we went for a fish but didn't catch any. So eventually Kev pulled out a jar filled with what looked like liver.

'It's my trade secret,' he said.

'Liver? What the heck is that?'

It turned out he had a jar of chopped-up liver soaking in kerosene. And he was catching fish, one after the other. I sat there with my mouth open, watching him do that, unable to believe what I was seeing. It wasn't exactly environmentally friendly!

As I've said, my Nan was one person who always understood me. Some years before her death, while visiting her in hospital, she told me, 'I've always understood you, boy. I've known all this time how special you are. We've all known, it's just that we haven't been able to cope or to deal with it. But you've got to stand tall.'

I think she could see dead people but was too afraid to speak about it. It's definitely something that's strong in my family, on both sides. Dad's really psychic. He always picks the horses but never puts the money on them! And mum's really spiritual. She's a reverend now, helping people pass over. Years later, when I came out and told my family that I was seeing people in spirit, because I didn't think there was any point in being dishonest and hiding, my cousins all said things like. 'Oh, mate, I've been seeing things forever … I've had visions … I've had dreams come true … I see things before they happen.' One of them, a professional hunter, says he 'knows' when there's deer over a hill because he sees redness, he just picks up on their energy. Another relative is a natural healer.

It took me until my late twenties to finally speak out about what I was seeing, and it was hard enough then. But when I was a young boy it was very, very confusing and after my Pop died I was not only very unhappy but I was having really bad dreams, nasty images, horrible stuff I couldn't understand. I went to pull the blinds down one night, five or six weeks after he'd passed, feeling full of dread of the Maori figures as usual, and Pop was standing out there wearing his favourite get-up – corduroy pants tied together with string for a belt and a checked shirt.

'These fellas are all right,' he said, 'and I'll tell you what they're saying.' Into the room they came with him, and he translated their journey, and what had happened and what they were trying to share with me. Although he was so close to many Maori people, Pop didn't speak Maori, but the spirit language is universal. When I've done readings, I've spoken with people from Korea, from Greece, from

Italy, from Croatia, who can't speak a word of English, through spirit interpreters. The universal language transcends all others.

The Maori people are incredibly spiritual; they believe in a vast number of gods, of the land, sky, forests, rivers, lakes and seas.

One of the most important places to Maori in New Zealand is Cape Reinga, at the northernmost tip of the North Island. They call this place Te Rerenga Wairua, the leaving place of the spirits, and Reinga itself means 'underworld'. As you look down from the cliffs in that sacred place, you can see the two oceans merging – the Tasman Sea to the west and the Pacific to the east. This is the final land-based site for departing Maori spirits, or atua, before they start their ancestral journey back to the homelands of Hawaiiki – the mythical, spiritual home of the Maori and all Polynesian peoples.

On the northern cliff face there is a pohutukawa tree, said to be at least 800 years old. Legend has it the Maori spirits use woven flax ropes to climb down to this tree, travelling to its roots and then to Hawaiiki.

When a Maori person passes they have to follow a hikoi, a spiritual journey to Cape Reinga, and they follow the streams and the paths of that journey all the way up in spirit. And at Cape Reinga when the moon and the tides are right, they cross into the next world. But the people in the area where I grew up were confined as a result of the way they had died. They hadn't crossed through. That's where Pop came through and helped me understand all this.

Many years later, after I had accepted my path in life and was more spiritually developed, I returned to Rotongaro and faced that stand of bush, and communicated with those spirit people. I at last fully understood that they were lost souls and that they didn't know how to set themselves free. I let them see how to cross through and so now they've gone, they've been set free. I think that's what they were trying to get me to do in the beginning, but I didn't understand.

CHAPTER TWO

A whirlpool of thoughts and feelings

ON MY fifth birthday I was all ready for my first day at school – happy as Larry, all dressed up in shorts and a T-shirt with a hand-sewn, fluorescent orange and black sleeveless vest over the top, and bare feet. It didn't bother me at all at the time, of course, but now I think, 'Oh my god!' With my little lunchbox in my hand I was very excited as I waited with my brother Murray for my first ride on the school bus.

The school we were going to was Rotongaro, a tiny country school about 3 kilometres down the road. The bus pulled up, I hopped on – and bam! I could feel everybody's thoughts. 'Who is this kid?' 'Who does he think he is, wearing that?' 'Look at his freckles!' And in my head I was thinking, 'What on earth are these people doing? Why am I feeling so bad about myself?' I just felt terrible, as though everyone hated me and I hadn't even opened my mouth yet.

It wasn't like being *in* everyone's mind, or actually hearing voices. It was that I could *feel* thoughts, all these swimming thoughts.

A way of understanding it might be to think of an electric fence. Sometimes, if you put your hand near the wire you can feel that penetrating energy. That's what it was like for me that day – it was more of a feeling thing. My heartrate went through the roof. And then when I sat down the pictures came; all the things that kids might think about. What kind of pushbikes they had. One had a Chopper and one had a Raleigh.

At such a young age I just didn't understand why I was getting all this. So as soon as I got my first bike, when I was old enough, I started biking to school – it was a bit more peaceful that way.

Even today, I find it difficult to go to a supermarket or, even worse, one of those large discount barns. If I walk down the aisles there are swimming thoughts everywhere – I pick up everyone's issues: what they can't afford, whether their husband's having an affair, if they'll be home in time. All this stress of thought in the aisles!

Have you noticed very few people talk to you in supermarkets, or will look away quickly if they catch your eye? It's because they're in their own little space, trying to work through their issues as they're shopping. They're focusing on releasing their stuff – and of course for me that ends up in a whirlpool of thoughts and feelings that I don't have any control over. I don't search for it, I don't look for it, but it's a vibrating feeling that I pick up on because I'm sensitive.

That's what was going on, on my first day of school. Being a country boy I hadn't been around other people very much, so this was a complete shock to me. Now I understand that this hyper-sensitivity, if you want to call it that – this ability to feel things and be sensitive to what's going on with people's emotions – is a bridge to connecting with people in spirit.

When it comes to feeling what's going on for a person who's passed over, the sensations are very minimal. As a comparison, if a physical human being's energy is a hurricane, the very subtle energy of a person who's passed away is a gentle breeze. I believe that many of my experiences in life have prepared me for understanding spirit. If I've had an understanding, or sensed the experiences of other people, then I can relate to the feelings that those experiences bring. I need to be able to appreciate those feelings – the vibe, if you like, that comes off a particular person in a particular situation – and that helps me to understand spirit even when the communication is very subtle and delicate.

But as a child, being around people, seeing spirit and sensing people's thoughts and feelings was very, very confusing for me.

To avoid it I separated myself from people, tried to stay away, which led to people thinking I liked to be on my own.

When I was around other kids I'd get really hyperactive, trying to shut out their thoughts and feelings, and so I wouldn't stop talking long enough to realise what I was saying. I was a bit of a rocket man – still am really – and wouldn't stay still for very long, because if I did I'd feel it. Sometimes even now, I'll go into a place where I find myself with too much going on, and I'll have to leave. That's one of the reasons I've always loved fishing – it gets me right away from everything and everyone.

One of my favourite spots to get away from it all when I was a little fella was to head across the grass at the back of our house, past where we kept pigs, and over the fence into a paddock that stretched downhill into a narrow gully. Down there, I was completely out of sight of our house, and in a world all my own. It was such a relief to be away from everyone.

I built a swing down in the gully and I'd just be hanging out down there, swinging on it, when people would appear. That predominantly happened after my Pop died. It might be someone's father who'd passed, or the grandfather. I might ask, 'Who are you?' 'I'm a friend.' What was I supposed to do? I was very confused.

They would say things such as, 'I'm the old boy from up there, you need to tell my grandson this, this and this.'

It was sometimes hard to do this, especially as I was so young, but I quickly learned that it was easier to do it than to have the spirit people come back, because they wouldn't leave me alone if I didn't do it. I did it subtly however, because if I had told the truth it might have upset people and they'd just end up confused.

One old guy used to come through to me – he was the grand-father of a boy who was a neighbour of ours and was really into his army models and planes. He had all these toys bought for him by his parents, but there was a feeling that his Mum and Dad didn't really care too much about him. They didn't have the time or the interest. His grandfather would come through and get me to ask the boy particular questions about his models and toys – to ask him how it was going because it was almost as if no one really cared what he was doing. The spirit of his grandfather would come to me in the paddocks and really he just wanted me to strike up a conversation so his grandson felt better as a person. Of course, I wouldn't run across the road and go blah, blah, blah, but I'd retain it and wait until I next saw him. I'd ask him, 'What are you building now and where are you going with that?' He'd talk and hopefully it would make him feel better. It wasn't about me at all, it was about healing him.

Looking back, I can see that so much of what happened in my childhood was about learning – learning to recognise feelings so I could communicate with spirit; learning what to do with visions. It was a mixture of scary – when the Maori tupuna were outside my window – and also, strangely, ordinary, because I really didn't know that everyone didn't have visits from spirit people.

I never considered telling my parents about my experiences, or at least I don't remember ever telling them. I had the strong feeling that they wouldn't want to know. In fact, Dad says I did mention a few times about my problems with ghosts, but he's always been a bit afraid of 'that stuff', as he calls it, and felt safer just ignoring it. But they always knew I was different.

As an older kid, I used to love swimming, and as we'd walk down the road to the swimming pool, I'd go into 'lala land' – 'the zone' is what I call it now – and I'd often think about what all the other kids' houses were like and what their parents were like. If I did ever get the opportunity to go to their homes, I'd say, 'Oh yeah, I already knew that!' I wasn't sure of what was going on but I just used to think I had a wicked imagination.

When I was six I very nearly drowned while on holiday in Whitianga, a beach town on the Coromandel peninsula. It's much more built up now, but in those days you could go down to the wharf and get scallops, snapper and crays off the boats – for just a tenner you'd get a big bag of them.

We were staying in our friends' bach and the grown-ups were getting themselves a bit drunk one evening. I left them to it and went down to the end of the wharf. It was dusk and there was a slight drizzle and for some crazy reason I slipped forward. I felt like somebody pushed me but there was no one there. I went over the side of the wharf and the tide was going out. When the tide rips through there, she rips through pretty quick. All I can remember is hitting the water, because it was icy cold, and being rolled around on the sand by the tide. I couldn't get back to the surface because I couldn't yet swim very well, and that's when the dolphins came. It may sound weird but I was surrounded by dolphins and had a very magical and powerful experience with them around me.

Luckily a teenager and his grandmother were walking up the beach towards the wharf. They were the only people to see me fall off the wharf. The boy was in his jeans and he swam in and dived under the water, found me and dragged me out of the water. I remember waking up as they were resuscitating me on the beach.

So while it may look like it was an accident that I slipped on the wharf and fell off, how did I really slip? I really felt like somebody pushed me, although there was no one there. I think I must have been meant to have that experience and perhaps it explains my affiliation with the sea. Even now, if I'm out in my boat and see dolphins, I say to my boy, 'Take the wheel' and I'll jump off the boat. I don't stop to think, or even care if I'm in the blue water out in the ocean, I'll just do it. It's a wicked buzz. They come up and look at you and click at you and it's just an amazing experience.

I've always had an affinity with all kinds of animals, something I have inherited from my dad, who has a special sensitivity with dogs. Animals are super-sensitive. You can communicate with them just through their unconditional love, but your intuition can tell you things as well. It's a very special thing.

CHAPTER THREE

'If you show me this why can't I make a difference?'

THE COMMUNITY of Rotongaro was extremely close-knit. Rotongaro Road winds its way around the farms, passing houses that are all quite well spaced out, but we knew everyone – we called our neighbours Uncle this and Aunty that.

Living in the country you make your own fun. We'd make mud slides and camp fires, go bow and arrow shooting, and shooting with guns, duck or pig hunting. The school would have pet days – I loved that. I put so much effort into making my lamb look sharp. It was the only thing I ever won. It was a great way to live your life, and I do think that one day I'll go back to living in the country.

I can remember standing up on a low hill behind one of our neighbour's houses. There was a small lake nearby, and in the early evening the swans would fly from that lake to another one further west. To a city-dweller, that sounds very picturesque; for us it was just fun. We'd stand on the hill and as the swans went overhead we'd be blasting away with the rifles. Aged 10 and unsupervised with a gun! We never thought anything of it, although Dad was always close by.

Rugby was a huge part of life – it was something everybody had to do. Dad was mad keen on it, and so we had to play it. I can remember playing rugby in my bare feet in the freezing cold. I don't like contact sports, never have.

My brother Murray was the rugby player and he made it to the Waikato reps and the New Zealand Colts, which is just before the All Blacks. He was a very good player.

Dad was a coach for the Huntly Rugby Club. He was a really good coach. He coached my brother's team most of the time and he and Mum took the team over to Australia to play three games in Sydney. That was a really big thing for my Mum and Dad, and they did fund-raisers for a long time, washing cars and all sorts of things with the kids.

As for me, I was a lazy little snot and I just didn't like playing rugby. That was one of the reasons I'd get dropped at my Nan and Pop's for the weekend, so they could all get on with doing their thing, and I could hang out with Pop, and later Nan.

But life wasn't always rosy in Rotongaro – some bad things took place. The worst thing – and this story is the answer to why I got involved with *Sensing Murder* – happened when I was about seven, and it taught me at that early age how murder can rip a community apart.

A lot of people ask me why I do the murder cases and the bottom line is I've seen at first hand the destruction that murder causes.

Pop was still alive then and he and my Uncle Kev were gathering at ours for a swan shoot. It was a community thing, and one of our neighbours from just up the road, Aunty Nola, was making quiches for a neighbourly get-together after the evening shoot. She wasn't my real aunty but we called her Aunty Nola because that's what everybody did and we were all very close. The mother of four boys, she was a lovely, placid person, married to Uncle Don, and she wore her hair in a bun.

She lived about 5 kilometres up the road. As we were gathering for the shoot the phone rang. It was Aunty Reenie, another neighbour who lived down the road, and she said, 'There's been an accident, Aunty Nola's dead.'

There was, as you can imagine, a huge commotion. Here we were, a community gathering together and socialising, and next thing there were cop cars and an ambulance flying along the road. This was a little country community where nothing happens. The most exciting thing in the day was usually when the milk tanker drove past the house and everything shook.

What had happened was shocking: A 13-year-old local boy, who like all of us lived along Rotongaro Road and who went to school with me, had turned up at the house to ask Aunty Nola if he could use the phone to ring his parents. He said he'd run out of petrol on his motorbike and because she knew him, it obviously wasn't a problem. 'Yeah, of course, come on in.' She carried on cooking, he went to use the phone, or to pretend to use it, and then he headed back into the kitchen, grabbed the cooking knife and stabbed her, many times.

Pete, her oldest boy, came home and found his mother dead in the kitchen.

It was a terrible, terrible time. I remember my mother collapsed on the floor – it just hit everyone like a tonne of bricks. The young lad who murdered Aunty Nola had said that he'd run out of petrol but when the police found his motorbike parked down the road, it was full. It was as if he'd planned it.

I was only seven, but even at that young age I was aware of what something dreadful like this does to a really close-knit community. We used to have what we'd call 'a bit of a do' down at the Rotongaro Community Hall, which is not even a kilometre from our place.

Everyone would go along and bring home baking – chocolate and shortbread. I used to go nuts for that food. We had great fun, but those stopped after Aunty Nola's brutal murder. They just weren't the same.

Of course the people whose son committed the crime were alienated and eventually moved away. I would've hated to have been in their shoes.

Even as a little fella I wondered how something like that could happen. Why would somebody hurt somebody in this way? Aunty was the most blessed soul that I've ever met. She was an earth angel, no doubting it, so why would somebody hurt her?

As my gift has come out stronger and stronger through my life, I've asked myself, 'If I'm able to see this stuff, then how can I help?' When *Sensing Murder* contacted me, the first thing I thought was, 'If it helps people then I'm in.' So far, it's been pretty good.

But there was another terrible event that was a further step along the way for me, in terms of being confronted with my psychic abilities.

I had a friend called Joe Kingi. He lived in one of the other council houses in our row of three. There was ours, and next door to us was the Hawiras, then a little bit of a depot where the council stored graders and stuff for the roadworks, and then the Kingis' house.

Joe and I used to knock around after school. We'd hang out and throw stones at each other, climb trees and steal fruit from the orchard and typical schoolboy things like that.

I was about eight or nine when I started dreaming of fire. All I could see was Joe's face in the dream, surrounded by fire. It progressed from being a dream into my waking thoughts; I just couldn't stop thinking about it. It was awful, but I didn't get it. I didn't understand that this was a vision of something that was going to happen.

Living in the country, we all had our own ways of getting rid of rubbish. We had an offal pit, a dug-out hole in the ground with a concrete slab on top that we used to dump rubbish into. It was pretty awful – Dad being the local dog man, we'd have dead dogs and all sorts dumped in there. The Hawiras, right next door, just had a basic hole in the ground at the back of their house – an open hole they used to pile their rubbish into and do a burn-off once it reached a certain height.

On this particular day the Hawiras had lit the fire and the smoke was billowing and it wasn't an issue – it was normal for us to see this. They were just burning their rubbish and had left the fire to it.

It was a Saturday afternoon and Mum was home washing the rugby jerseys. That was Mum's thing – she washed more rugby jerseys than I care to remember. She'd do my brother's team, plus other teams where the mothers couldn't help out because they were too busy on the farms. This particular day she was doing our sheets as well.

Unbeknown to us, young Joe decided to go and play by the fire. He'd found a canister lying around at the depot and thought he'd throw it into the fire. It turned out to be an oil filter or a fuel filter of some sort and, of course, as he was watching all the flames and stuff the canister exploded.

There was a hell of a bang, a really big explosion that shook the houses. And then I heard Mum screaming and she'd jumped the fence into the Hawiras' garden with a wet sheet that she'd snatched off the washing line, because she'd seen Joe being blown out by the force of the blast. The next thing I saw was Mum wrapping him in the sheet – in those days we had a ringer washer so it was actually quite wet – and Dad was there too. They turned the hose on and dowsed him in the pure cold water, literally just trying to keep him saturated. All his skin was coming off his face and all over his body.

Eventually we got him into our car to take him to hospital. It was terrible, all the screaming and witnessing someone's skin melting like that. It's a horrific thing to remember. One of the cases we did on *Sensing Murder* was about 19-year-old Blake Stott who was found burnt to death in his car in South Otago. I was a mess afterwards as it brought back a lot of memories for me.

Thankfully Joe survived, but he wasn't the same person afterwards. He spent months in hospital and the doctors all said that it was the swift action of Mum and Dad that had saved him. I remember going back to the hospital to visit him and he was on morphine and incoherent. We went back again and I'd collected lots of pine cones to get some money to buy him some lollies so he was happy.

I really struggled with that afterwards. I don't think it was that I felt responsible, but I just didn't understand. I'd seen the fire on his face for a couple of weeks prior to the accident and I couldn't stop thinking about it. When I saw the smoke I didn't piece it together; I didn't even know he was going to be there.

I was being given these pictures in my head but didn't know what I was supposed to do with them. I didn't blame myself, but I just had these big questions: 'Why?' And, 'If you show me this why can't I make a difference?'

I know now that there's not really a 'why'. It's just visionary – I see stuff, and I can't own everybody's experiences.

I trust this part of my gift now – if I see things like that now I tell people, especially if it's somebody I know. If it's somebody I don't know then I use it as training for my vision. If my son Javan's going to get into trouble I'll say to him, 'Mate, if you do that, there's a possibility that you're going to hurt yourself.' 'Yeah, yeah, yeah.' 'All right, so you'll learn, right?' 'Yeah, yeah, yeah.' And then something happens. 'Oh okay, I learnt the hard way, Dad.'

We can't, as parents, be responsible for our children's choices and it's the same for others – we're not responsible for their actions.

Looking back, I realise that many of the stories I remember from my childhood are to do with this journey of self-awareness and learning about my gifts. As a child, I couldn't put it all together, but later on when I finally accepted myself, I could see it all for what it was.

When we were younger Mum and Dad didn't have a lot of money, but they worked really hard all year to try and give us a holiday. When I was about nine, we had a fantastic family holiday at the popular seaside town of Mt Maunganui. It's much more crowded now but back in the late 1970s, it was much quieter. We had some great times there, as you do, kids running wild at the beach.

I loved being in the open spaces by myself, so on this particular holiday I'd get up really early in the morning, about 5 a.m. or 5.30 a.m., and wander down to the jetty with a bucket of pipis I'd collected the day before, a ball of nylon and a couple of hooks. I'd be fishing away – catching and releasing the fish, just enjoying a nice quiet time. I loved being beside the sea, it was just fantastic.

One day, at about 8.00 or 8.30 a.m., a father and his kids came down to the wharf. They put a bucket down beside me and I began to have these incredible pains in my body. My arm felt as if it had been smashed in a vice, I felt really sick in my stomach and I couldn't understand what the heck was going on.

I said good morning to the dad and as he was standing next to me I felt his sensations go through my body. Because I wasn't feeling well I thought I'd better go home to Mum. I walked off the jetty and started walking up the road for about 50 metres, when I came right. I couldn't understand what had happened, what was going on, now I felt perfectly fine. So I thought I'd go back. But as I started getting closer to the father the sensations began again. Instead of staying or parking next to him I said, 'Gidday, I've changed my mind, I might go down the other end there.' When I went to the other end of the wharf I was all right. As soon as I came close to him I started feeling it again. As a child this was really puzzling – I knew something was there, I knew it was something to do with him. It wasn't until later on in life that I realised that when I meet someone and experience something like that, those feelings are not mine, they belong to the other person.

31

In that case, looking back at it, I think he'd probably broken his arm as a child and may have had a pin in his arm. The stomach pain could have meant he was hungover for all I know.

So what happens now is if I'm meant to feel it, because we need to discuss it, then it will come out. If somebody's had their arm broken I'll be able to tell you which arm and usually how.

Back then though, it was very, very confusing. It was easier to stay away from people.

CHAPTER FOUR

Understanding my faith

ON NIGHTS when the moon was full, which meant the tupuna did not come out of the bush, I would open my blinds and stare up at the stars. It was so cool. I'd gaze up at the sky and I'd talk to God, or the universe, whatever you want to call it, and I'd ask, 'What's out there? What's the point of me being here? How does it all work?'

From the very beginning I felt like a stranger in this world – a foreigner in a small town. I believed then, and now, that my home is in the stars and that one day I'll return there. I'm not scared of going home; I'm looking forward to it. But I am here until my service is done.

When you think about things and talk to God, the answers might not come in the way you expect, but they will always come somewhere along the line, providing your eyes are open, and you're not blinded by expectation. It's really important to understand that it's not just a matter of *getting* an answer, but having your eyes open to see it.

I think spirits were trying to teach me to understand faith from when I was very little.

Life itself comes down to experiences. When you're born you don't know who you are. As soon as you're born you forget where you come from, where you've been and all those sorts of things. Your job initially is to understand who you are.

When I was little, I struggled with reading and writing. I'm dyslexic and in those days it wasn't understood, so I was just marked out as dumb. Teachers may as well have put a cone on my head and shoved me in the corner, and so I was incredibly frustrated and felt useless right from the start. The moment I set foot on that school bus I thought, 'What's the point of being here, I want to go home.' And for me, home is in the stars. I put my trust in that.

When I was little and asked the stars, 'Why have you sent me here?' the spirit people all used to say, 'You've got to share what we've given you.' And I never understood it until later on in life. We all have the answers to life inside ourselves. It's whether you want to go dig it out or not – whether you're ready for it, and prepared for the truth from within.

It was also during my early primary school years that I learnt to astral travel. It started when I was dreaming one night – the kind of dream that we all have every now and then, where I was falling off a cliff, but before I hit the bottom I woke up. It freaked me out, so I decided that if it happened again I would stop myself from waking up, and I'd take control of the fall.

When it did happen again, as I was falling almost to the ground I yelled out 'Stop!' and I did – about a foot off the ground. It was an amazing feeling, being in charge of my dream.

I then raised my head up and took off – over the top of the cliff, across the tree tops and over the sea and the mountains … looking at people and cities, bright lights and places I'd never seen or even heard of. It became almost a nightly event.

I still use it regularly, and can astral into my past, my future and even into other universes, or astral travel to heaven to visit my mates.

I used astral a lot in the *Sensing Murder* show. That's how I'd know where and how things had happened, and the bits and pieces within a crime scene.

I have been known to describe the layout of people's homes and what they are wearing.

Astral travel is a very powerful gift yet some people use it for negative things and this is dangerous. But used in the correct, positive way, it's amazing. I love it. It makes me feel like a bird – absolutely free. When bad stuff happened to me I would put myself somewhere else with the gift of astral travel … It's just learning to be in touch with your mind, body and soul at the same time.

As a child, of course, this was a very private part of my life that I couldn't talk to anyone about. I was experiencing sights and dead people, visions and astral travel, but without any understanding of why.

I can look back at those experiences now and appreciate that they were symbolically significant, even if they were painful and confusing at the time. One such example was at school at Rotongaro when a boy I was a little bit friendly with, although he was a couple of years older, lost his rag over something. I don't think I was being cheeky. Maybe I'd just beaten him to the top of the hill – it was that sort of scenario.

He got me up against a grass bank, and he literally just stood there and whipped me really badly with a length of alkathene, the black pipe that they used to whack cows with.

I couldn't figure out why he would be so angry or aggressive towards someone who'd done nothing.

I quickly understood the scale of feelings in a situation like that – the difference in sensation between someone being calm and placid, and someone who's aggressive and murderous. I understood what it felt like to be on the receiving end when I was trying to be positive, and what it's like to be overpowered.

But the biggest thing was that, as he was hitting me, I was watching his eyes and I could see his aggression, but I could also see the pain that he was experiencing at home.

Pictures were coming in to my mind of things going on behind the scenes, and what I was getting was pretty severe. It turned out that his Dad used to beat the living daylights out of him. I see pictures of this kind like a movie or a TV screen, as if you've put it on fast forward. I could see and understand things about his life and why he had so much aggression inside him.

Poor bugger. He was a nice enough kid, but he'd snapped and lowered himself to his Dad's standard. However, the last I heard of him, he has a couple of kids and he's doing really well so I hope he broke the cycle of violence at some point which would've been his job to do while he was here in this life.

Nothing can take you over unless you give it the power. I could've been negative about being whipped by that kid with the plastic pipe, but instead of being a victim I wanted to learn from it, so I did. Seeing his pain and aggression helped me recognise the significance of different kinds of energy. I began to understand that there are two lifestyles – positive and negative – and I can now recognise those feelings in people when I meet them. If I'm doing a reading for somebody whose father beat them with a belt, I'll pick up on that sensation. I've experienced it and I understand when that vibration comes.

I compare the energy I get off people to being like music. When the nuns play their angel music it's absolutely peaceful, and when the Buddhists chant it's empowering and uplifting and refreshing and positive, and I feel really good and clear and at peace with everything. If you listen to Marilyn Manson, however, you just want to kill people literally. They're at totally opposite ends of the spectrum.

When I was seven, our home life changed dramatically. Mum left us in Dad's care and went back to studying at Waikato University. She'd spend all week in Hamilton and came home for the weekends. As an adult, I totally understand her need to do that. After all, she'd left school at 13 and obviously wanted to make a better life for herself. But as a child, I felt terribly rejected. I was struggling at school, being treated as dumb by the teachers, and as just plain different by everyone else. I really needed to have her around and I found those years very hard.

But by the time I was about 10, in standard 4, the last year of primary school, she had qualified as a teacher and was working at Huntly Primary School, about 20 kilometres from Rotongaro. So I switched to that school as it also included the intermediate classes, Forms 1 and 2. I'd go in with Mum most mornings, or sometimes bike all the way myself – I'd still do anything to avoid going on a school bus!

I had a wonderful class teacher there called Mrs Pickett who realised I had dyslexia and that was why I couldn't read. It took all that time for someone to figure it out.

Within a couple of days she had picked up that something was wrong. 'Look,' she said to me one day after school, 'I've been watching you and this is what I think the problem is. You're not silly, you're not stupid, despite what everybody's led you to believe.'

And I just felt so happy because she understood. It was a relief more than anything.

'It will take some time but we can get through this together,' she said to me. She was a lovely lady. Apparently she changed a lot of people's lives. She certainly changed mine.

Mum would have to stay after school to do her meetings and stuff and Mrs Pickett would take me for extra reading and teach me how to get through. She must've had the patience of a saint because I was really clever at avoiding the subject.

Mrs Pickett was a good sort – she was strict but she was really good. I still had a lot of knockbacks, though. Some of us aren't designed for the sort of stuff you have to do at school. When I really tried but was told it wasn't good enough, it felt like I was constantly being kicked about. At the end of the day, though, I've done all right. You don't need to be educated to be successful; you just need to follow your dreams.

Not that I had dreams then. I didn't really care about many things by that stage.

I must have been 10 when we went on a school trip to Auckland – the big smoke for us Huntly Primary kids. We visited the big factories where they made Steelos, and the Apple and Pear Board. We stayed at a place called Knock Na Gree, at Oratia in West Auckland. It's an old Catholic retreat, I've learnt recently – there were certainly a lot of crosses around. And it's probably really beautiful, set in the native forests in the Waitakere Ranges, but at the time I thought it was one of the scariest places I had ever been.

That was caused partly by the difficulty of being around so **many** other people and their spirits, especially at night, and partly by the history of the place. It was exceptionally busy – full of spirits wanting attention.

I didn't want to sleep in the dormitories with everyone else – there were too many dead people, every kid had spirits hanging around, and I knew there would be just way too much action. But we were allowed to sleep in tents, and my friend Chad asked me if I wanted to sleep in his.

'Oh cool, what sort of tent?' I asked. And he said, 'It's an Indian thing.' I was up for it, anything to stay out of the dorms. Then he brought out his tent and it was literally a sheet with an imprint of an Indian on it.

You simply put the pole up and there was no ground sheet, no pegs – it was a complete disaster. Of course there was no flat land, it was all hills, but we were really brave and tough and pressed on with our plan to sleep outside.

So eventually I was lying there in my sleeping bag, and I could feel I was surrounded by people outside of the tent – dead people, that is. I eventually got to sleep just by humming to myself. I often used to do that. When I woke up a bit later in the dark, however, I wasn't in the tent. I was at the bottom of the hill on the bush line surrounded by people who were trying to get me. It was the scariest thing I ever experienced as a child. There were all these spirit people reaching out to touch me – there were people, faces, coming in from all directions. I was absolutely petrified. I didn't know what to do with myself. I was frozen in time.

I think I must've passed out in fright, because I didn't want to get out of my sleeping bag and run, there was no way in hell that was going to happen. Chad and I ended up staying in the dorm after all, but that was another story in itself. The dorms were very busy, active places as well which was just too much for me. The whole trip was a nightmare.

I remember playing a game where we had to walk through the bush to go out to the playing grounds and I was sent back for something, a rugby ball probably. It was the middle of the day, but I just didn't want to go. Of course I had to, but just walking from the playing fields, through the scrub on the track to the dorm was the worst experience. There were dead people, everywhere. There was a statue of an angel which turned into a gargoyle, a really demonic face and I was totally petrified.

Back home Mum and Dad asked, 'How was camp?'

'I just hated it.'

'Why?'

'Because it was horrible.'

'Why?'

But I was too scared to say anything.

I believe that these spirits were what we call the lost souls. They weren't necessarily bad. They could just have been people who had passed over and they just didn't want to accept that they were dead, so they were stuck. When someone like me popped along, who was only a kid, I was seeing them, but what was I supposed to do? I was only 10 years old.

CHAPTER FIVE

'Why have you sent me here?'

THAT YEAR was my last year at Huntly Primary. When I was 11, Mum and Dad decided to send me to a private boarding school in Hamilton. That might seem like a surprising decision, given that we were by no means wealthy, but there were a couple of reasons. One was that I'd been pushing for it on account of what I'd heard about the fourth form programme at the school, which meant six months out in the bush – a real Outward Bound kind of scenario. It sounded like bliss to me, and I was really keen to do it.

Secondly, Mum and Dad were struggling with where to send me for my college years. They didn't want me to go through a public school because of my difficulties with dyslexia. So, after much deliberation, they decided to send me as a boarder.

It's an Anglican school, and Mum was saying, 'Yes, well, we're Anglican! We were married in an Anglican church.' And Dad was like, 'Like hell we are, we're not bloody Anglican, we've never been to church …'

It is a blue ribbon school – very expensive, enormous grounds, with most students coming from very wealthy backgrounds. Hamilton is New Zealand's fourth largest city, sitting in the basin of the Waikato River – the 'mighty Waikato' – and is surrounded by fertile farmland. The city has a historical character as 'cowtown' and a lot of its wealth originated with conservative farmers. The school drew on those wealthy families, and also the businesspeople making money in the city, and from all over New Zealand. It was all an extremely different social environment from Rotongaro.

Dad at the time had an old Ford Falcon, a big, old blue tank, which made a real hooha of a noise when he started it. We turned up at the school on my first day and found ourselves amongst all these hobnobs. I'd never seen anything like it. I had my little case with my clothes and uniform, which I hated. Dad put the bag out of the car and he said, 'Righto, boy, see ya later.' He flicked the key over in his ignition and the car made that almighty noise and I was like, oh no! Dad was cracking up and doing skiddies out the gate. He just put his foot down and buggered off. And that was really the end of my time living in the country.

Pretty much from the beginning I was incredibly unhappy at boarding school. The bullying was terrible. All the third formers had to be what they called a fag to a prefect, just like in the old English system. It meant you cleaned their shoes, you folded all their clothes, you made their beds, you got them toast when they said, 'Get toast'. There were times when you had to lie in their bed in the winter, freezing cold until you'd warmed it up and then they'd come and kick you out. You were like a hot water bottle for them.

Everyone just decided to pick on me, I don't know why, and everything went downhill.

I think it really annoyed them that I didn't fight back – 'keep knocking me over, pal, but I'll just keep getting back up'. I wasn't being a martyr or anything, I just didn't see the point of lowering myself to their stupid standards. It was the same as what happened when I was younger, and I just thought, what did I do to deserve this?

Being in the boarding school dorm situation was a bit like being in the army. You had to do this, do that, do your chores, polish that, be at dinner at this time. But when no one was around the boys used to play up, they'd do dumb stuff, steal stuff off each other, cut each other's clothes.

One night, I was sound asleep in the dorm when my duvet suddenly flew off and some of the boys began whipping me with wire coat hangers. That was one hell of a journey, because I couldn't stop them. There were about four of us that they did it to, but they stuck with me. They didn't stop when it came to me.

Even without the bullying I found those dorms extremely difficult. I didn't like sleeping with other people in the room. It was really busy with constant whispering of other people's spirits that I couldn't make sense of – boys' parents or their family or their people coming to look after them. I could pick up all their dreams; their downloads.

Dreams are a dress rehearsal for life, where your spirit or your inner self shows you what's really going on. If you had a dream about running away from something negative and weren't aware of the role dreams play, you'd just think you had a really crazy dream. But if you are aware of their importance, you can decide to take control of that dream – ask yourself what it means and stand up and face your fears. It signifies you're probably running from something in reality, and standing up to it can change your whole life.

At school I'd see the other boys' family members standing beside them or sitting next to them on their bed, and their downloads – just their own heads and thoughts and their things happening. Spiritually it was quite intense for me.

Meanwhile, the bullying got worse. One day, I went to the sick bay to see the nurse. I think I had the flu. In the waiting room were a couple of boys who had been particularly nasty to me. They saw the nurse, then left, and I was still sitting in the sick bay waiting for my turn. One of the boys went around the outside of the building, swung open the sick bay window and just pelted me with a grapefruit, smacked me in the head with it. Everyone was laughing, so I stood up and picked up the grapefruit and just at that moment the nurse came out. She of course wanted to know what was going on.

'Miss, they just threw it at me!'

They were called back in, and we were all given the same punishment – what they called a 'workout' – by the prefects. It was a tradition where the prefects of your house took you to the gymnasium and made you sweat. Some of the things we had to do included standing with our backs against the wall, knees bent out in front, nothing underneath. The prefects put a weight on our laps and we had to stay there. That was okay for a few minutes, but then the burn started to hurt. And if we moved they'd put on another weight. The more you moved the more weight you got. They did it until they felt like you'd had enough, you couldn't take it anymore.

So, we'd collapse and then they'd do some other things. One of us would have to start running from one end of the basketball court and one at the other, and if we were caught up by the other person we were pelted by balls and sandshoes and other stuff as we were running around. Basically it was a licence for the prefects to beat the daylights out of us. If we were caught by the other person it was just terrible, really bad – we were made to climb the rope and again they would just pelt us with balls. They would kick them, they wouldn't throw them gently. Baseball balls, hard balls not just soft ones. And if we didn't make it to the top of the rope we'd fall off, so just had to keep going. If we didn't do our press-ups properly or whatever they'd just kick us in the ribs. It was just shocking.

I ended up in the sick bay as my body was totally black and blue, like I'd been beaten up to a pulp. I was just broken, literally broken – it had been a terrible combination of physical violence and psychological terror. The prefects actually got into so much trouble that they outlawed these workouts throughout the school, because of the beating that we'd taken that day.

Mum was passing through Hamilton and called in to see me in the sick bay. She wasn't too happy, and if I remember correctly she started something off, and that's how it got banned.

It took a while for Mum to realise just how bad it was for me at boarding school. I remember calling her on the phone, bawling my eyes out.

'Mum, I just want to come home, you know, this is just shit.'

'Oh, you know, toughen up, you'll be right, this is just part of it, you'll get through it, it's just homesickness, you'll be fine.'

She wasn't being cruel, she was just trying to make me feel better. But she didn't see the side of it where they were so horribly cruel.

I was labelled a 'homo' – the putdown back then for gay people. I'm not gay, but everybody got a label as soon as they got to the school. They'd look at you and they'd go, right, you're a homo, that's it. Or, you've got curly hair so we'll call you frizzy.

I don't know whether it was because they could tell I was different, or just because I was gentle, but I was labelled a homo and everybody used to beat me. I copped it every time. I'd be walking to class and someone would just punch me in the head, for nothing. It was just really, really tough.

They'd steal food off us – I couldn't even have a meal without somebody disrupting things, kicking my chair as I tried to eat soup. I know I'm focusing on all the bad stuff, but I hated it, every second of it, and I didn't want to be there. For me that label of being gay was the catalyst for everyone to beat the daylights out of me, whether they knew me or not.

Finally, there was an incident where two fifth formers held me down and burned me with lighters and wires and stuff. I've still got scars on my legs from it.

After that, and also because Mum and Dad had moved to Hamilton, I stopped boarding at the school at the end of the third form and became a day pupil instead.

Before I started high school I'd been one of Huntly School's best swimmers – Martin Chadwick and I were always very close competitors – and I'd won medals for swimming. When I moved to boarding school I really wanted to get into the sport, and so I did. But my first swim was against this guy who was the best swimmer in the school. His name was Colin and he was a couple of years older than me, and I beat him. So he and his friends beat me up and said, 'If you come back to swimming we'll do it even worse.' That was the end of my swimming career. And I had had hopes to be a really good swimmer, a competitive swimmer.

I remember telling this to my mum, at the end of the year probably, when she asked why I hadn't done swimming that year. I told her the story about Colin and she saw red. Soon after that, we were at the beach and me and some mates were walking around, with Mum and Dad behind us. Colin just happened to be walking towards us with his mates.

'Oh, Cruickshank, you little homo.' Boof! And he punched me on the side of my head. But, of course, my parents were just behind, and Mum just bowled through and confronted him.

'Are you Colin?'

He was petrified, but he replied, 'Yeah.'

She grabbed him by the scruff of his neck and gave him a right telling-off.

We were all completely stunned. But he never touched me again, never laid a finger on me after that.

CHAPTER SIX

Standing my ground

AS THE third form wore on, I just tried to keep a very low profile. With my head down, I didn't speak to anybody and became very reserved. I just didn't want to be there. I kept the peace, but trouble still seemed to find me.

One of my teachers was a man I disliked on sight. He was one of those people who seem all very nice on the outside, but was real nasty on the inside. One day, he called me out when I was in class.

'Cruickshank!'

'Sir?'

'Out.'

I thought, 'Oh, what have I done now?' I hadn't done *anything*. I was just cruising.

He said, 'Come with me' and took me across to the library. In the library was a book that had been defaced with obscenities, really

47

profane stuff. It included things that were derogatory to Christ, demonic talk, what they would do to the nuns, all those sorts of things. This teacher had decided that it had been done in my handwriting.

Now, I never went to the library because, being dyslexic, the library was the last place I ever thought of going.

But he said to me, 'Cruickshank, you did this.'

'Sir, no I did not.'

'Cruickshank, I know you did it, admit it.'

'Sir, I didn't do it.' This argument went on and the teacher ended up standing over me, foaming at the mouth.

'You damn well did this.' He was really nutting off at me. I just stood there and was crying because I was so scared.

'Sir,' I said, 'I did not do that, I would not do that, that is not my way, I would never write something like that in somebody else's book, I don't even think like that.'

Can you understand what it's like to be blamed for something that you haven't done? It's a horrible feeling, makes you sick. But the teacher kept telling me, 'You did this, you did this, you did this, admit it, admit it.' He couldn't break me, couldn't get anywhere, so he took me to a corner of the outside quad and made me stand there at attention.

'Don't move.'

It started to rain. I still had to stand there. Then I got called to the headmaster's office.

'Kelvin, what's going on? Did you do this?'

'No, Sir, I did not do that.'

And then he said, 'Well, I've got your school work here, and the writing matches, and it appears to me that you have done this.'

'Sir, I did not do that.'

In the end, because they couldn't solve who did it, and they wanted to expel the culprit, they did employ a writing expert who confirmed it wasn't me. The writing was similar but it wasn't mine. There was

Right: Fishing in Whitianga.

Below: Pet day at Rotongaro Primary. I was very proud of my champion lamb. Probably ended up in the pot.

My uncle Kev, my brother Muz and me. Dolly the ute in the background.

My pride and joy – my Supermax BMX. Dad's Falcon is in the background.

Monty Haack, my Pop.

A classic school photo –
Rotongaro Primary.

Happy after winning a swimming competition at Huntly Swimming Pool.

My Dad Les and me the day I went to boarding school. I look happy . . . yeah right!

huge pressure put on me which caused a lot of emotional torment. Yet, nobody said sorry. The teacher barely spoke to me in class after that because he had been proven wrong.

My point to this story is that when I know I'm in the right, I won't back down. When I'm wrong, I'm happy to admit it and apologise. It's the way I've always been.

This has been an important point with *Sensing Murder*, too. When I do a murder case, when the spirits tell me to say something, then that's it, and I stand my ground. In the first series that we did, I'd get the message through and the production people would say, 'Well that doesn't make sense.' I'd just think, 'I don't care if it doesn't make sense to *you*, it makes sense to *them*, so that's that.' And then the response would be, 'Oh, I'm sorry, we realise that now that we've done research.' That's what they would say weeks after the shoot.

So those experiences at boarding school really taught me to stand my ground, and I think I learned how to be strong. Those experiences made me who I am. It was absolutely disastrous at the time, but it was something I needed to go through. Spiritually, it was a huge learning curve.

At high school we'd have almost daily religious instruction – church every day. Like most boys, I found it really boring, although it could also sometimes be very peaceful. And I used to sit there, saying to Jesus, 'If you are there, why aren't you helping me? If you're there why don't you stop this?'

But then I went through a process of understanding: maybe it was because they needed to teach me something. Because when somebody who has been beaten up by their dad or by their boyfriend, or whoever, comes into my space, I can feel what they did – someone standing over me, being aggressive. I notice it straight away and I'll say, okay, this is what's happening, let's work it through. And we talk about it. My work's not just about reading and talking to dead people; it's about counselling, to a degree, to help people understand that it's okay to go through these things but it's not okay to hold onto it. So it was a leap forward in my understanding.

What I realise now is that I chose the experience in order to understand what it's like to feel the hurt and to be able to stand on my own two feet without lowering myself to other people's standards.

It also taught me to understand why people were so cruel. I realised their behaviour wasn't my problem, it was theirs – their insecurities, the fact that their dad beat them up or the fact that their mummy or daddy would buy them anything they wanted but just push them into a corner. So, the aggressiveness or assertiveness of those school bullies came out because they didn't know where else to put it. Nobody wanted to listen to them. Some of them were just unwanted souls.

Sometimes, I lower myself down to road rage, who doesn't? But then I realise, what's the point? It's just wasting energy on something that can't be changed. But I *can* change myself.

Despite everything that happened in the third form, I was still hanging out for that fourth form experience of the adventure school survival program. And sure enough, it was the best thing ever. There must have been about 50 of us, in the middle of nowhere – in a well-known state forest – and I just had a terrific time. We had to cook our breakfasts and our dinners and were supplied with lunch. But you had to learn to survive, that's what it was all about. Survival school. We hunted, tramped, kayaked, abseiled and sailed.

A highlight was the 48-hour solo. All we had was what we were wearing – shorts, boots, shirt, jersey, swannie. We were given 600 millilitres of water, a handful of peanuts, two slices of bread, a little cube of cheese and a carrot. And our sleeping bag. There were no knives, no matches, no pens, no papers, nothing. We were taken along on a tractor and the instructors said, 'Right, Cruickshank, get off.' And then they'd drive down another couple of hundred yards, and drop another boy. We had to make a rock pile so they knew where we were, and then pace out 50 steps into the scrub to build our shelter, our bivouac, out of whatever we could find. We'd been trained to do this.

The forest is full of deer. On the second morning a stag came and stood right beside my bivouac, roaring, while I lay in my sleeping bag. It was a huge stag, a 14 pointer.

Pop was hanging around keeping me company, so it was sweet as. That's why it was peaceful for me to be just chilling. I felt completely safe and I mostly just slept – we'd been on the go for a couple of months, and I was pretty exhausted. But I also had lots of different dreams and visions that seemed irrelevant at the time but which ultimately ended up happening – things like seeing a restaurant with a sign and lights flashing out the front that a few years later I ended up managing. That sort of thing has happened all my life.

I climbed a tree at some point, straight up from where I was, to see the view. That was pretty cool – although I'm scared of heights so that didn't last too long.

I was determined to have my two days in the scrub completely honestly, without cheating. Some of the guys left their bivouac and went out to the road, hooked up with their mates, and hung out. Some of them just couldn't handle being alone. I think there were only about three or four of us who actually made it by ourselves. I stayed put and wanted to be completely solo for that time, to show myself that I could do it. So, I was really proud of myself. It was an incredible experience of self-discovery.

There was one freaky experience that happened during the three-day team solo, which was when you went out with two friends, for three days, with nothing but your clothes, raincoats and a packet of matches. There was no food at all, no water, no sleeping bags, nothing, just a packet of matches. It was pretty tough. I remember having raincoats because it pelted down the whole time.

We made a bivouac with ferns and other stuff we found, and were all crouched in there together. It was freezing. When we got the fire going it just smoked, and all the wood was soaking wet. And there was water dripping on us like Chinese water torture. It was just driving us nuts. We were so cold we were all cuddled up. We had no choice. There we were in a pair of shorts and a raincoat with a swannie underneath, freezing our arses off, legs ice cold – it was just horrid.

I finally dozed off, and I know this is going to sound really weird, but the side of the bivouac opened up and a face appeared. It looked like one of those ancient shrunken Maori heads, as clear as anything. It was looking at me, not saying anything but just looking. I was petrified.

I thought I was just dreaming, but when I woke up there was a hole in the side of the bivouac – a hole the size of a head in the exact place I'd seen the head. It was as though somebody had forced their hands into the fern walls and parted them. The bivouac was thick with about 20 ferns, upside down and round about and all over the place. You couldn't penetrate it, even with your own hands. If you tried, it would just spring back, and yet there was a hole, not perfectly round but enough for somebody to put their face in and look at you. It was really weird.

I still don't understand what happened, but I do know that that presence wasn't somebody that I knew. It must have been somebody that spiritually belonged in the area.

CHAPTER SEVEN

'A black shadow was holding me down'

IT WAS in my fifth form year, when I was 15, that my spiritual crisis really began to deepen. It's hard to explain what life was like for me up till then. Seeing spirit was just so much a part of my life, but I still didn't understand what I was seeing, and in a bizarre way it just seemed quite normal. I never told anyone about it – I just kept moving.

I'd be looking in the mirror in the school toilets, for instance, and I'd see not just myself but several other people as well – not people I knew, but perhaps they must have been boys from the school who had passed on, or visitors from the cemetery down the road. In any crowd of people, there were always extras. The spirits would always try to chat but I got clever at blocking them out. I would listen to loud music, or walk away fast, or turn my back on them and try and focus on other things such as the people I was with or the area I was at. Distraction was always the issue, and that's why I always kept myself full-on busy, no time to think, just hard-out work.

By the fourth form I'd made friends with a great guy called Steve – he was a ginga, a redhead, so he used to get hassled too. We became really good mates, especially after we got back from the fourth form adventure school. We always used to sneak out – we'd skive off out of the school grounds and go and smoke a Rothmans or Winfield Red. Disgusting, eh? Man, we must have stunk.

But having a friend made school a lot easier. We just hung out together, went down to lunch and kept to ourselves. During school holidays I stayed with his family. Mum and Dad were having trouble. But I didn't really understand it, and I spent a lot of time away from home.

When I'd boarded at school I literally wasn't at home that first year. In my second year I was home but we were like ships in the night. For most kids a school day would be from 8.30 till about 3.30, then they'd go home and do their homework. I had to be at school at 7.45 a.m. for church. Then after lessons all day there would be training for whatever sports you were doing. If you were doing three sports you had three different training events, if you could schedule them in. I was playing hockey, volleyball and squash.

I then had to get on my bike and head home to do all my homework, and by then it would be nine o'clock at night. Then I'd get up and do it all over again, five days a week. Kids have it light these days. If we didn't do our homework – holy sugar. So, I really didn't pick up on a lot of Mum and Dad's issues. I knew that they argued. My reading of it is that they were just totally different people, oil and water. I don't think either of them did anything wrong; I just thought they'd be happier if they weren't married. Mostly I just felt excluded from what was going on in the family. My brother protected me a lot, but I was hardly ever home, and I'd felt different all my life anyway.

Then, one evening it was a full moon and I was sitting outside on the lawn underneath the stars, still in my school uniform, and Mum came out to talk to me.

'Son, I want to talk to you about something.'

'Oh yeah?'

'I don't love your Dad anymore.'

'I kind of felt that, Mum,' I said.

'Well, I just want you to know that we're probably going to split up.'

'Oh,' I said, 'well, that might just make you happy, that's all that matters.'

The next thing I knew there was a horse float at the front door and she was packing up and had gone. And I was left thinking, 'Where did Mum go?'

I don't remember any talk about what I was going to do – she just left, and I was really, really angry. I wasn't angry because Mum and Dad had split up – I thought that was good – I was just really angry because I didn't know where I stood. I was 15, it was the start of my School Certificate year, and I had raging hormones, chemical imbalances all over the place.

So I just hit the drugs – heaps of pot – and got really stoned. I just didn't care anymore, and was desperately trying to push everything away. When I think about that time, the word angry comes to mind, because I was really struggling with my own sense of self.

Spiritually things were also becoming very difficult. It felt like I was being pinned down spiritually. I'd be asleep and it felt as though somebody was sitting on top of me, as if they'd pinned me with their hands, their knees. A black shadow was holding me down and I couldn't breathe, I couldn't scream, I couldn't move, I couldn't do anything. It was horrible.

It started to happen quite regularly, and after Mum left it got stronger and stronger. When you have spiritual abilities there are two sides to the coin – positive and negative. The positives are great, but you've got to learn the negative is there too. It's called psychic attack, where negative spirit energies hold you down and they even try and enter your system, which is a really freaky experience.

It's an energy form that's trying to get into your zone, your being, which is not nice. But the one thing I learnt pretty quickly was to use something I remembered from school. It was a Bible passage: that it's not my way, it's thy way.

There was another quote from the Bible about asking the Lord for support when in time of darkness. So I used to use the Lord's Prayer to help that darkness go away. And it used to, eventually.

That's why, even today when I do my seminars, I tell people about the value of affirmations and prayer. It doesn't matter what affirmations you use, as long as it makes you feel good. If you can recite that whole affirmation without a break you're sweet. If you're reciting an affirmation but your concentration is broken and you start thinking about whatever's going on at work, or you start going off into la la land, then that negative vibration's still with you. You must recite, recite, and if you get cut off, start over. When you can repeat it, one time after the other, that clears that negative vibration from you.

So that's how I learned that, when I was 15, because life had just become so dark and I didn't want to be there anymore. Even despite the affirmations, I couldn't always hold the negativity at bay. It might work for a few days or weeks, but then – slam! – the darkness would come again and I'd be fighting.

It was a very dark time, which lasted right through the whole School Certificate year, and the year after that. I really bombed out, and when I went into the School C exams I just wrote my name on the paper and a smiley face. That's how angry I was. I was full of 'I hate the world'. It was stupid, but I had no one to talk to about it.

After that, I was taken out of that private school and sent to Fraser High School, a local co-ed state school, to do second-year fifth. I hated every minute of it.

I had no friends, I knew no one, and I just kept asking myself, 'What's wrong with me, what's so wrong with me?' When people looked at me I knew what they were thinking. 'Stupid.' And, 'Oh, that's the new guy'. They instantly had something against me. I didn't want to get into any sports because I was too embarrassed or too shy. I did eventually make a few friends but they were the baddies. I went to school, signed in and then I left. I was smoking pot around that time, too.

I set myself up to fail at the school and on my sixteenth birthday in March 1987 and only a few weeks after the school year even began, I was asked to leave.

So there I was, 16 and out of school and really confused. I got a job as an aluminium joiner, making windows, but of course I was really just a lackey, stacking things up, sweeping floors, picking up after the men. I knew I wasn't in the right place, but I hadn't yet learned to trust my feelings about things like that.

I remember biking on my ten-speed to that job one freezing cold morning, just three or four days into the job, and going over the handlebars. I had no gloves on and was badly grazed across my face, hands and chest. I was in absolute agony. People were driving past and they just sort of looked at me. No one seemed to care. I sat there thinking, 'Am I not meant to be going to this job?' 'Is somebody trying to tell me something?' And then I thought, 'No, you're just nuts, get going, come on, hurry up.'

These days, if I'm getting the signs that things aren't right, I listen to them, absolutely. Recently I was out near Great Barrier in my boat and the weather blew up really rough. I thought we should tuck in behind a Channel Island and do a little bit of fishing. Every time I put my line in the water, it broke. Now, I never get broken off. I'm a fisherman, I know what I'm doing. When I went to tie the knot and the knot kept coming undone I stopped and said, 'Right, guys, we're out of here now. I'm getting all these signs and I need to go.'

As a teenager I saw those signs but I brushed them off.

I did that job for a month, but in the end I got sacked because I didn't have my driver's licence. My initial thought was how was I going to tell Dad. He, my brother and I were all living at home in Hamilton. I got back to the house and I said, 'Oh Dad, I lost my job.' He just went off his scone.

'It's all right,' I said, 'I'll get a job, because I want to be a chef anyway.'

I'd always liked to cook, from when I was a little fella doing the spuds for Mum, to being at school camp and cooking breakfasts and dinners out in the open. When I was at Fraser High School, home economics was the one subject I really nailed – I topped the class. It was really cool having something I was good at because I still couldn't read properly. Also, I knew that cooking made people happy, and that's what I somehow knew I was here for, to try and make people happy. Even if it came at a high cost, such as working long hours, missing birthdays and events and weekends. Weekends? What are they? Chefs just don't get them.

I was sacked on a Wednesday. The following day I went downtown on my pushbike and walked into a restaurant. It was a Cobb and Co, a family restaurant chain – a good place to learn the basics. I had to start somewhere after all.

'Can I see the head chef, please?'

It just so happened to be the head chef that I was talking to, a lovely Irish woman.

I said, 'Look, I'm really keen for a job, I don't care, I'll mop floors, do whatever, I'm young and I'm enthusiastic and I really want to be a chef.'

'You come back on Friday,' she said. 'You go and get these things here,' and she gave me a list. So, with what money I had left from the other job, I bought a pair of white pants, white Bata Bullets, a white T-shirt and a white apron and hat.

I also enrolled in the cooking programme at Waikato Polytech, so I was working and studying – anything to keep busy, keep moving, running away from my spirituality.

I got my first tattoo then too, primarily to annoy Dad. He'd always maintained, 'Get a tattoo, I'll scrape it off with a wire brush.'

So I got a peace sign on my ankle. It really hurt too. I forgot about it, until six months later I had my feet on the coffee table, drinking a beer. Dad came in from having a few beers at his mate's house or something, and instantly spotted my tattoo.

'What the hell is that?'

'Oh, yeah,' I said laughing, 'I did that ages ago to piss you off. Ha ha, sorry, I forgot about it, Crookie.' Crookie was Dad's nickname, everyone called him that.

He said, 'Right, I told you,' and the next thing I knew he was out in the shed rattling around. And my brother said, 'Man, I think he's getting that wire brush.'

I took off out the door and sure enough, Dad was out there with the wire brush, shouting, 'Come here,' down the driveway. Lucky he couldn't catch me, jeepers creepers, I reckon he would have rubbed it off.

While externally it looked like I'd sorted out my stuff, inside I was just really depressed and sad. I felt I had no one: Mum had gone; Dad was angry; Murray was going through his own issues. All of them were completely wrapped up in their own dramas. And when you think about it, I'd only just turned 16 so I was still a kid, even though I was out of school and working. I was trying to be really tough about everything. I said things like, 'Oh, cool, my parents have split up', but I was just evading the issue and becoming sadder inside. I had the feeling that I didn't fit in anywhere, and more than anything I felt scared.

All the feelings I'd had my whole life of being different, the battles I was waging against that darkness that just kept attacking me – it all got too much. It was exhausting and I just wanted out. One night when I was in my room by myself, I began slicing at my wrists.

I'd just drawn blood and I thought, 'Yeah, I'm going to do it.' I was quite calm. Just then, my brother's girlfriend walked in and said, 'What are you doing?' I'd been busted. She told my brother, who told my mother. A couple of days later she turned up at tech in my lunch hour, and I was there still with the bandages on my arms. She had arranged some counselling, so I went and saw this guy who sat there looking over his glasses. And he taught me one of the most valuable lessons of my life. He said, 'When you get home at the end of the day, visualise all your issues, all the dramas that are stuck on you, on your shirt. When you take your shirt off, throw them in the washing machine with the shirt.' Now, that I can do. I can visualise stuff like that, and today if I do a show, the first thing I do when I get home is take off my shirt. Let it go.

So that was very worthwhile. But of course I couldn't talk to him about any of the real stuff that was going on for me – the spirits and the darkness. I'd spent a whole lifetime dodging school bullets, so it was easy to say what he wanted to hear, and after two or three sessions he told Mum I was sweet as.

He couldn't have helped me in that other way. I don't think anybody would have understood that. I didn't tell him anything about myself spiritually because I knew that I would be in trouble.

CHAPTER EIGHT

'I should have known; why didn't I know?'

THUS BEGAN some of my craziest years out of a pretty crazy lifetime. I was working 60–70 hours over five days at the restaurant, and doing two days at tech studying to qualify as a chef, so there were no days off.

It was a big relief to be out of school where I was always in trouble, and always on detention. At polytech, nobody gave a stuff about the students – you just did your thing and it was fine; you had freedom of expression.

In that first year of tech I was paired up with Mark – he was a nice guy and we hit it off. We were both out in the field and putting ourselves through tech – as a team we cooked really well and would be finished three times faster than anybody else in the class because we were both working and the others weren't.

His nickname is Gonz or Cherrydog, and we're still friends today – he's been a big part of my life. He knows more about heavy metal than anybody – he's got collections, he's got the badges on his jacket. I don't like all types of heavy metal, but I like loud music because it distracts me from all the busyness around. Gonz had a motorbike, and by that stage, I'd also bought one, so we'd go cruising together. That was pretty cool. I still love motorbikes today – I've got a 2006 black and pearl Suzuki Hayabusa GSXR1300, the fastest factory-production bike on the planet and I love her to bits.

I never stayed long at a job because I'd just get bored. In my second year of polytech I left Cobb and Co and went to another restaurant. A younger guy called Hamish began working there as a dishwasher but he wanted to be a chef. He was a nice guy, a loveable rogue, and gorgeous looking – girls just fell off him.

He said to me, 'Kelvin, I'm going to get a tattoo.'

'Oh yeah, choice,' I said, because I had a tattoo and I thought it was pretty cool. But he came back with a grim reaper tattooed on his arm and I said, 'Mate, why did you do that?'

'Oh, because nobody cares about me.'

'What's going on?' I asked.

And he said, 'Oh, f*@k everyone' and was really agitated and upset.

After that I noticed Hamish's behaviour becoming really reclusive. We went to tech together and ended up hanging out with a few of the boys from a couple of other restaurants who smoked heaps of pot. But things just weren't right with him and he wouldn't talk about it.

One day we skived off down the pub at lunchtime, and had a beer. Choice. Just one beer, no worries. We got back to tech, and he said, 'I'll just go to the loo, bro.' So, I cruised back into class. But Hamish didn't come back so I asked the chef if I could go and check on him.

He was lying on the floor of the toilet. He'd taken a tube of bicycle glue and literally sniffed the whole lot up his nose. It was terrible to see my mate lying on the floor in that way. I picked him up off the floor, sat him up, checked him, and then got permission to take him home in a taxi. I dropped him off, sweet as, no worries. And not long after that he went into his Dad's room and shot himself.

When somebody says to me after someone takes their life that they didn't know what was happening with them, well you're not meant to know when somebody's going to do that. When they're talking about it and they're being loud about it, then they're not going to do it. It's the quiet ones that you've got to watch, really watch them closely because if they tell someone it will spoil their plans. It turned out there were lots of things going on in Hamish's family that were pretty bad, but we just didn't know about it. He just didn't feel loved. I loved him, he was a good guy.

I kicked myself for ages after that, saying to myself, 'I should have known, why didn't I know?'

I learnt from it, though. I can now look at somebody who comes into my room for a reading, and I'll know if they want to kill themselves, because I'll get that same feeling I had from him. It's just that I didn't understand it back then.

Suicide is a very complicated situation to be in. When you're drug-free, completely clear-headed, and that's what you do, you take yourself out, then that's your journey, that's what you were meant to do. So, as harsh as it sounds, your soul had to learn – your destiny has been fulfilled.

When you're using drugs or alcohol however and take yourself out, no matter which way you do it, your destiny is not being fulfilled and you're breaking the universal law by taking your life with your own hand. Usually when we pass, we have our spirit relatives and friends waiting for us to show us the way, but if you pass from suicide involving drugs or alcohol they won't come for you. You may be lost in a limbo period for a certain amount of time – if you were 20 when you killed yourself, you may have passed, say, 68 years before you were meant to. So for 68 years, our time, you're lost. And it's not a nice place to be lost in. There is no love, nothing. I call it the lost world, the nothing-ness. I've seen people who've passed from suicide on P, for example, step out of their bodies and say, 'What have I just done? Oh no.'

Before Hamish died I was using a bit of pot. I just didn't have a way of expressing myself, and so I used a little bit of anger, a little bit of self-hate, self-doubt, self-abuse in some instances with drugs. In truth I hated smoking pot. I only did it to fit in, and because it was part of my running away from who I really was. But the visions I was having were so clear and so frightening that it was just not good for me; it made me worse.

I became extremely paranoid and felt disgusting. I knew that I was better than that. And then I lost Hamish, and most certainly learnt the hard way about drugs.

I was broken up by Hamish's death – I didn't want to get close to anybody. I just put my head down and got busier and busier. By the time I was 18 I was head chef for a guy who owned two smorgasbord restaurants in Hamilton and Palmerston North. I was flying between them, with no days off. It was very full on, busy and intense.

Even though I was so young, the owner got me into training his staff. I'd been showing some other young guy how to do something, and the owner said, 'See how much he's learnt in the short space of time you've been here?'

'Oh, yeah, I didn't think about it like that,' I said, and had a sudden realisation that this was what I was good at. I love teaching people stuff, love sharing knowledge. I get quite excited by that, and still get a real buzz from doing that today in my workshops.

At one point around then I also had a job in a factory making plastic bottles. I'd work from 3.30 p.m. till late at night in a restaurant, get to the plastics factory at midnight and be there till about 6.30 a.m.; go home for some sleep during the day, and then do it all again. I made stuff-all money, but it wasn't about the money. It was about keeping moving. It's a drug, in a way, that kind of overworking. Because I felt nobody cared, I'd just keep working. Obviously you can't have friends when you've got that sort of lifestyle, so I was spending a lot of time on my own.

For a while I went and lived with Dad in Ngaruawahia and worked at a beautiful restaurant attached to the RSA. We'd do bistro meals and buffets with an à la carte restaurant attached, and I used to run all that. I'd go home in the afternoon between shifts, supposedly to have a sleep but of course I wouldn't – I'd play with my slug gun or ride my motorbike around. And then I'd go back in the evening. I did that seven days a week, constantly.

Dad and I fell out and I went back to Hamilton, and got a job at a really cool café called Nuts and Crackers. This was a turning point for me. I began as just the third chef, but I didn't care, I just wanted to cruise and do dishes for a bit as I'd been working so hard for so long. But then they asked me to do some salads, so I said, 'Yep, sure,' and they said, 'Man, that's pretty good!' Then the head chef left and I got appointed to his job – and the place just flew.

We had bands coming in every Wednesday night, and amateurs could turn up and have a go – play their harmonica and sing some songs, whatever. I play the harmonica, so after work I'd ride home on my pushbike at ungodly hours of the morning, playing my harmonica all the way home. It was a really cruisy good time.

By now it was 5 November, 1992 – the night before my life changed. What a night that was – crazy! Gonz and I used to go to the Chartwell Tavern every Thursday, but I was always late because of my work. So I'd get there late and everyone was usually trashed. I normally didn't drink very much – Two-Can-Kel is what I was called – but this particular night I thought I'd try and catch up with them. So, there we were at the Chartwell Tavern, a pretty bogan pub, drinking shots, getting trashed.

The pub closed and Gonz, myself and my flatmate, Podgy, literally carried each other out to Gonz's Morris Minor van. We called it the

Hell Van and had turned it into a bit of a shaggin' wagon – we put carpet all around it, put pillows in. We were just young dudes being silly buggers more than anything.

I think we must have spent at least five or so minutes trying to put the key into the lock. We were very drunk and acting pretty stupid. We all got in the car – Podgy in the back on the mattresses, and Gonz and I in the bucket seats up front. We were driving home and there was a sharp corner coming up. I warned Gonz.

'Corner?' he said.

'Yeah, the corner, man, it's, you know, *there* … oh no, look out for that pole!' Boom. We smashed the van into the kerb, up into a power pole, bounced off it and kept going down the road. We got onto the river road in Hamilton, and up and over the hill and turned a right into my street. The steering was so gone we couldn't get it up the drive.

We eventually fell out of the Hell Van and just left the car, because we were all laughing at our narrow escape. If he hadn't turned when I said, I would have been totally munted by that pole.

We got inside and carried on drinking – it was Guy Fawkes, and we had fire crackers and sky rockets and Gonz fell through the garage roof and made a big hole in it. It was a terrible night.

The following morning, Gonz called in sick but I had to go to work. I'd placed an ad in the paper for a part-time chef, and had job interviews to conduct that day. I met a few people and was thinking that I really didn't feel good. And then this girl walked in and I knew straight away. I didn't know her name, hadn't looked in my list for her yet, but she walked in and I went, 'Hi.' And she went, 'Hi.' And that was it. Click.

They talk about chemistry, but it was even more than that. Spiritually, I saw these wee lights coming out of her, and little lights coming out of me, and they met, smack in the middle, over a counter. And I knew she was the one.

I asked her, 'Are you here for the job?'

'Yes, my name's Rachael.'

And I just went, 'Oh.'

Because the amazing thing was that when I was seven I had the knowledge that I was going to marry someone by her name, and here she was. I checked on the list of applicants and sure enough, there was the name 'Rachael' – but I'd been so hungover I hadn't noticed.

I didn't give her the job – I couldn't, because I knew I wanted to date her. Instead, I got her a job at my mate's restaurant. We started seeing each other, and it wasn't long before she moved into my flat.

CHAPTER NINE

One in a million

AT THAT time I was living in a really cool house in Harriford, which is quite a nice area of Hamilton. It was a big brick house overlooking a reserve, set in the bush and very quiet and private. How that had come about was a strange little story.

I was on my way to work one day when I saw a girl stopped at the lights in a Mini, and it was obviously not going. Everyone else was just beeping at her. I was on my motorbike, so I parked it on the side of the road, ran across with my helmet on and asked if she was all right.

'I can't get my car started.'

'Oh, well I'll push you off to the side of the road.' I'm not mechanical, but I had a look around and there was a blown fuse but there was also a spare fuse. I put it in and away she went.

This was near the beginning of my time at Nuts and Crackers, and a couple of days later I was looking for a flat. I went through the newspaper ads, picked one and gave it a call. I went around to have a look and when I pulled up outside the house, guess who answered the door? The girl with the Mini. It was karma. I'd helped somebody, a stranger, on the road and then soon after I was knocking on her door and she gave me the flat just like that. Because she knew I was a good person.

Actually, I wasn't too sure about the girl, but I really needed a place, so I moved in. However, it wasn't long before the landlord realised she was selling drugs from the property and asked her to go, and I took over the lease. I got a flatmate in and we had great parties but really looked after the house. I was there for three or four years, all up.

Spiritually, through this time, it was still much the same: the weird dreams, seeing spirits, and always feeling different.

Sometimes I'd be in the restaurant in the late afternoon, around five o'clock. It'd be quiet, no one else around, just me, prepping for the evening service. I'd go outside for a cup of coffee, and just sit there, looking out over the city, and I'd watch people going home and I'd often wonder what it would be like to be normal.

Because I wasn't normal, I knew that, and my life didn't have that normal structure of regular daytime hours. There was a song by Guns N' Roses called 'One In A Million'. It's on their very first album. 'You're one in a million, you know that you are.' I always felt one in a million, I always felt *different*. That may sound completely strange, but it's certainly not an ego thing, it's the way I felt.

When I met people for interviews I knew straight away what sort of person they were, what kind of character they had – whether they were a thief, whether they had a temper. It came over really strong. That's why I was really good at picking staff and could suss out people, defuse issues, all that sort of thing.

So although I see, hear and feel spirit, it's not always about dead people, it's more about learning to understand people, about yourself, why you feel this way.

The most amazing thing that I have ever seen, spiritually, happened when I was living in that house in Harriford and Rachael was at work. I was sitting on the grassy bank one afternoon and the sun was dimming down and I wanted to write a story. At school I used to like to write short stories but I couldn't spell and I couldn't express myself easily in that medium, and it used to frustrate the heck out of me. But on that afternoon I thought I'd try to write down my thoughts.

As I was sitting there on that bank, I swear this white light path came out in front of me, and I started walking on it. I walked up through the clouds and I walked and I walked, and I was thinking, 'What am I doing?' I was writing this all down at the same time as I was seeing it, visualising perhaps, if you want to call it that. But the physical aspect of it was I could actually feel the steps and all the sensations of walking up this light path, up through the clouds and through the change of temperatures and into this big white light. Then, lo and behold there was my grandfather standing there.

'Hey, Pop, what's happening?' I asked. I looked around and there was a big corridor to the right and a big corridor to the left, a huge, beautiful fountain, chequered floors, black and white. Pop said, 'Hi,' and then disappeared.

There was a big staircase that spiralled up behind the fountain. This person started walking down the staircase and I remember seeing the sandals, just the sandals and the feet, and there was a long, purple robe that came down to the ankles. I tried to look up, but I couldn't, and I think I wasn't meant to.

I was overwhelmed. The feelings in that environment were unconditional love to the fullest: no pressure, no judgement, no hatred, no anger, no violence, nothing but safety. Complete safety. Protected, nurtured, humble, compassionate. It made me feel so good.

'Hey,' I yelled out, 'Hey, who are you? What do you want from me?'

71

But he didn't say anything, and I asked again, 'Who are you?' And I got no response but then I got a really strong sense of the word 'thus'... And the word was *thus* ... and then I was sitting back on the grass wondering what had just happened.

The sun had gone down. It had been about four o'clock; now it was just about dark, so I'd been a couple of hours at least in this conversation, in this path.

I found that piece of writing some years later, and I sat there crying because I finally realised what it meant – that I had been on a journey home, and I believe I met Jesus Christ, if only for a moment. To me that was massive, it was a journey of return. They were saying, 'We're trying to show you that you can do this.'

Now I teach meditation, or share knowledge of meditation, and take people to that place, first. Then they can go through the corridors and visit their family, their dog, their cat, whoever. They can go into other corridors that lead up into places of healing for people with cancer, to places where souls can rejuvenate, or if they've been abused in some way they can go into another corridor to release those things. It's a healing place, and there are just so many facets, it's incredible.

Jesus Christ is still a huge part of my life. I see him often, and he is very meaningful to me. I see his face appear in walls or on the floor when I'm reading in shows. His face appears on people's shirts, on their clothing. I see that silhouette, the familiar shape of what he's been portrayed as, that's all it is. And when it comes, I know that there is a need to say 'Jesus Christ loves you'. For the person that I'm drawn to saying that to, those few words are everything. Sometimes I get up on stage and I have moments like that and I wonder how I'm going to keep this under control because it is just truly amazing.

I know there will be people from the Christian faith who feel what I do is wrong, but I've never understood that. Some say mediums conjure up people's spirits from the pits of hell and stuff like that. But what I do is just another facet of spirituality.

There are many different aspects to the established Christian church itself. There are manipulative churches where people are required to give large sums of money to the pastor or risk going to hell. There are other churches, such as the one my own mother ran at St Paul's in Paihia – also called the Stone Church. You go there and you just feel the love. She doesn't say, 'Give me, give me, give me,' like an evangelist does. You can see the difference: one is a manipulator; one is doing good.

It's a well-known fact that church attendances are dropping off. It's obvious that people are looking for other ways of expressing their spirituality, and of understanding how life works from the spiritual dimension. I believe in Jesus, and I've been helped greatly at times by Christian beliefs. I still use Christian prayers as affirmations and as positive forces in my life. So, that's why I'm not knocking Christianity. It is a free choice. However, I also see and communicate with dead people.

It's a wonderful, God-given gift that brings enormous happiness and healing to people. Jesus talked to people. Moses did too. John did. Peter, Paul. I believe they all had these abilities.

Jesus was a master who, allegedly from what scripture says, was able to communicate with God. I talk to God every day. Do you? I give thanks for my meals, for my friends, for everything good in my life. I get on my bike and I say, thank you.

Some people judge me before they understand. It doesn't matter if you're a Christian or a scientist or a guy working for the post office; if you judge my spirituality before you understand the experience then you deny yourself something that could potentially be an incredible experience in your life – the most amazing miracle that you have ever had.

That afternoon on the bank by my house I still had a long way to go. But that journey up the path of light was a very significant event, because what I'd done was I'd sat still for five minutes – something I'd been avoiding all my life, and in that quietness, my gift was able to manifest itself, and I was shown that incredible path. While it was still going to be another few years before I really understood or accepted my gift, I did begin the process of questioning myself, and of acknowledging my abilities with spirit.

CHAPTER TEN

'The Circle of Life'

I WAS still a very young guy, just 21, and trying very hard to grow up and do the right thing. At the same time that I was becoming more conscious of my spiritual gift, I was also head over heels in love. From very early on in our relationship I loved Rachael and wanted to marry her, which was amazing for me because I was a person who used to run away from people.

After we'd been together about a year and a half, she became pregnant with our son – that was a miracle, and I knew she was pregnant. I saw Javan's face come through, and knew instantly that he was there. Sure enough, a little while later she said, 'Oh, I'm pregnant!'

I proposed to her and said, 'Babe, I love you and let's get married and try and make a real good go of it.' When her family stepped in and tried to organise the wedding and it was beginning to look complicated, I said to her, 'Babe, we'll just have a little barbecue and get married and that will be that.'

So that's what we did. We had no money but we didn't care. We just wanted to get married and we did. It was really nice.

Ever since I'd met Rachael, I'd been determined to try and make a go of things, which meant finding a new job, one that paid better. Unfortunately, the job I found threw me right back into the cycle of being overworked and exhausted.

It was in a popular Italian restaurant, where I was employed to make the desserts with the promise of advancing to entrees and mains after six months or a year. Well, guess what, after two weeks I was head chef – the Italian owner, who had also been the chef, hurt his hand so he got me to step in, and he saw my potential pretty quickly.

He just said, 'I'm boss, I don't need to work, I've got my chef. I stay and teach, that's it.' So that was that. But he was a real hard character who liked to do things his way. Nine and a half months was the longest stint I ever did without a day off and that was where I did it. After that I said to him, 'Mate, I'm having a day off.' And the reply I got was, 'No day off for number one chef.'

The work was constant, but I did get looked after. He'd say, 'Hey, it's the chef, look after the chef. Hey, what you want? You want clothes, you want this, you want that? What do you need?'

He was a law unto himself, this guy, he used to eat *glass*. If he'd had some wine he'd chew the wine glass, crunch, crunch. Those really thick ash trays? Crunch, crunch.

In most restaurants in those days, the early nineties, you just chucked stuff in the microwave. We didn't do that, we cooked real Italian food, in pizza ovens and pans. And we had people lined up outside our restaurant, two to three hundred covers in one night. We'd work from seven in the morning till one in the morning, every day. It was crazy. But it just got to the point where I'd become really unhappy. I finally took one day off, and Rachael and I were at home and we were saying to each other, 'Oh, it's so good to be home and to be together.' Then we heard a car come up the drive, and it was the owner.

'Babe, hide,' I said, 'because he's going to try and get me to work.'

The front and back doors were open but there was no time to shut them. We locked ourselves in the toilet. The owner came knocking on the door, and then through the house.

'Keluso' – that's what he called me – 'I need you to come to work, where are you? Come on. I need some help, we very busy, yah, yah, yah.' He walked through the entire house but he must have thought that we were out, because he didn't find us. Finally he got back in his car and drove away.

Rachael and I were both so exhausted then – she was working hard in the industry too. It's a hugely tough industry, and some people just use you. Trying to stand up to somebody like the owner of the Italian restaurant was really difficult, especially when I was trying to make everyone happy. But I had to say no. It's a hard lesson I learnt through my career as a chef, that 'no was no', and that was that.

In the end I just said to that owner, 'Look, I'm not coming to work, I'm done. Pay me out.'

I was glad to be out of there and enjoyed a bit of time off. But I walked out of the frying pan into the fire when I was offered a job running a new restaurant, as an executive chef, setting it up from scratch. It was fun, but it ended up being 80–90 hours a week.

I was getting paid something like $400 a week, on the proviso that after four months I'd get a percentage of the total gross profit. So I put in seven days a week to get the place up – I built it up really well, the place was pumping and people were queuing up to get into the restaurant.

At this time, Rachael was pregnant, which I was extremely happy about. I had trained my staff to cope without me during the birth, and everything was ready for the day I'd have to take her to hospital. She went into labour, so I rang up my boss and I said, 'Look, I've rung all my staff, they're all ready, I'm taking my wife to the hospital, everybody knows what they need to do.'

77

And this guy, this owner, said, 'Can't you just drop her off? I need you here in the restaurant.'

'Whoa mate,' I said. I was really shocked. 'I don't think this conversation should be taking place. I said I'm not in today, all my staff are covered, they all know what's going on.'

'I need you here,' he said.

'Look, I'm sorry,' and I hung up the phone.

I took Rachael to the hospital, and we had our bubba. Javan was born on 15 September, 1994, at 3.15 p.m. at Waikato Hospital. He weighed 6.15 pounds and was just totally adorable, and as he was being delivered, the background radio was playing Elton John's song 'The Circle of Life'. Wow, talk about sparkle – I don't think I'll ever forget the amazing feelings, but I guess everyone says that.

His name is from a book of biblical names that Rachael's family had given us. We were struggling to decide on a name, so one evening I instinctively suggested that we close the book. We held hands and let it fall open, and the name Javan, halfway down the page, glowed and that was it. It means to make wine, in Hebrew.

After he was born, I went and had a meal with my mum, and then went into the restaurant to check on the staff.

Soon after that, two weeks before the date I was supposed to begin sharing in the profit of the restaurant, the owner said, 'Oh, you ran out of guacamole, this is unacceptable behaviour, this is your first written warning.'

I was gobsmacked. 'What's your game? We did four hundred meals last night, we were going to run out of something. We whipped it up, not a problem.'

'Unacceptable behaviour, not having to stand for this, blah, blah, blah.'

I thought that was a bit on the nose. Two days later I'd run out of bacon and was ten minutes late, for the first time ever – and was given my second written warning.

I looked at him and said, 'You're only doing this because you know you owe me loads of money. I'm getting a lawyer.'

'Get out of my restaurant.'

'Fine. See you in court.' Two years later, I got him to court and I won.

He was a nasty piece of work. He took all my ideas, and he robbed me. I'd worked for months knowing that I was eventually going to get paid well, and I ended up with nothing. I had a six-week-old son, and no way of supporting my wife and my child.

I had to go milk cows. It wasn't a pleasurable experience. It's the worst thing I think anybody could ever do, but my brother-in-law got me the job, and I certainly needed the money. Then, two weeks into that, my brother-in-law gave me a litre of milk, because we had none in the house for a cup of tea, and I put it in the car and took it home. But the owner of the farm saw him doing it, and we both lost our jobs, and I wasn't paid for the work I'd already done. The boss was right, we should have asked, I totally accept that. But it was very hard at the time, and all for taking a litre of milk.

To cap it all we were then burgled. We came home, Rachael, Javan and I, to find nothing left. I'll never forget coming home, pulling into the drive and before I could even see the house, I just said, 'Oh, no.'

'What's the matter?'

'Oh, something's not right.'

'What do you mean?'

'Something's wrong, someone's been here that's wrong, it's not good.' I felt it.

'You don't know what you're talking about.'

'Yeah, something's not right.' As we pulled into the carport I could see broken glass, and I said, 'Oh, no, please don't.'

Some gang prospects had burgled our house and taken everything, even food out of the freezer. We had to laugh at that because Rachael had frozen some breast milk, and they'd taken that too. That would have been interesting. They'd smashed the goldfish tank, the TV, the pots, they took clothes, and they went through our drawers. It was a disgusting feeling, a violation. I didn't care much about the materialistic things, but the violation of our own sanctuary, and the fact that we didn't have much anyway, was very upsetting. The only thing they left was the baby's room. They didn't touch it.

Dad came out and bought us a jug, because we couldn't even make a cup of tea. They were caught, eventually, a year later.

I was 23 years old, Rachael was 21, Javan was six weeks old, and we had nothing. I'd lost two jobs and now we'd been burgled. To be honest, I don't know how we survived, I really don't. I know that my Dad came and helped, and Rachael's family helped out and bought food and stuff.

We were extremely lucky in one way – we'd only bought insurance two weeks earlier. I'd never had it before. It was weird, but it must've been spirit looking after us.

CHAPTER ELEVEN

Playing psychic games

THROUGHOUT those years, I was, as I've said, becoming a little more aware of my gift, and a little more aware of strange things happening. In some ways, I was playing games with it, testing myself out.

I'd do things such as ask myself how many covers we were going to do in the restaurant that night, and see how close I could get. I was usually either on the mark or one or two off it. I used to play games with my staff, and ask them who could tell what a particular table would order. I always used to win.

'Um, I think the lady over to the left is going to have the lamb, the guy's going to have the fish.'

My staff would say, 'The guy's not having the fish, he'll be having the steak.'

But when the order came in, the guy would be having the fish, the girl the lamb. We used to just do fun things like that.

I'd always know before I even got out of bed if any of my staff weren't going to come to work. I'd think, oh, such-and-such isn't coming to work today. I'd get to work and the phone would go, 'Hey, Chef, I'm not coming to work because we've had a family bereavement.' Those things still happen to me today.

There was one instance that was really funny. I was working in Rotorua – this was some time down the track – and my sous chef said, 'Morning.'

'Hey mate.' And then I said, without even thinking about it, 'You know, you must have had a fight with your wife because you didn't mow the lawns last night after work.'

He stopped what he was doing. 'How did you know that?'

'Oh, I just had a thought.'

He looked really angry. 'What do you mean, had a thought? Were you watching me? What were you doing, coming around to my house, watching me and my wife fight?'

'Dude, not at all, I just had that thought. Maybe we should talk about it. Are you all right with that or what?'

So off he went and talked about his wife, how she expected him to do this and do that. He looked at me after he'd had a talk about what had taken place and he said, 'You know, I feel so bloody good now. Thanks, man, for listening.'

All it took was that trigger of me getting the picture in my head that he'd had a fight with his wife because he didn't mow the lawns. It obviously helped him get some stuff off his chest about the demands she was making on him, even after he'd worked long hours. He went home and talked to his wife and they had a big hui, a big meeting about things, and got their relationship back on track. Now, that wasn't because of anything I did, other than spark him to talk.

It took me a while to realise that a particular feeling came over me when I played those psychic games, or acknowledged those 'thoughts' that popped into my head. It was a positive feeling, not a negative one. I just felt safe, warm and fuzzy when I started doing things like that, and it just got stronger and stronger and stronger, which was really cool, and that was the start of where I'm at today.

Also, as always, bad things happened if I ignored those feelings.

On Guy Fawkes the year after I'd got together with Rachael, we had a huge bonfire out of dead bush and other stuff we'd built up throughout the year. Mates came down from Auckland and from all over the place and we had a big party. It was raining, and had been for a week. All the wood that we'd built up for the year was sodden, so we tried lighting some tyres and that didn't work.

We were pretty happy, had a few beers, and came up with the idea of siphoning a mate's car to get some fuel, just for a laugh, to get the fire started. It was Guy Fawkes, for goodness sake!

My mate Craig went down to put the fuel on and I suddenly said, 'Man, I don't think we should be doing this.' We were getting closer to this big heap of wet wood, and I said, 'Nah, mate, it's just not good. It's not good at all.' I was getting flashbacks to my childhood, really strong, and I wouldn't go anywhere near it.

'It's all right, it's not even going man, it's not even going,' Craig said, and the next moment the whole thing went boom and blew up. He went flying, and so did I, and all you could see was light. It was a really freaky feeling. What had obviously happened was there must have been an ember somewhere from all our attempts at lighting it, and the petrol just hit it and that was that.

Craig ended up in the creek with a few cuts from the trees and scrub. We got him inside and he was as black as the ace of spades, just covered in stuff. So was I, but not as bad as him. He didn't get burnt, which was really, really lucky. But that overwhelming feeling of, don't do it, don't do it, don't do it, was why I'd backed off.

Those things started happening more and more and I started feeling those sensations when I was in the restaurant. We used to make this stuff called blackjack, which is sugar reduced until it turns black.

We used it for stocks and stuff, to colour them. I was going to pick up the pot one day, getting a towel ready and I kept hearing, 'Don't pick up the pot.' I *had* to pick up the pot, I had to take it from point A to point B.

So I picked it up, took two steps and it splashed against the side, hit my hand and burnt the skin off it. It was a pretty serious injury.

These days I've learnt to listen to those voices that are coming, I believe, from my higher self, or my intuitive side. I'll ask whether I should ride my motorbike today and the message will come back, 'No, not today.' So I'll take my car. But if the message comes back that it's safe to take my bike, sweet, I know I'm going to be okay.

Being out of work was very stressful as I didn't know how I was going to provide for my family. We didn't have huge bills by any standards, just the basics, food, rent, etc. But it was pretty hard as a young couple, living on one wage.

At the same time, the hours I'd been working – often 18 a day – meant I was extremely fatigued, and so the more hours I did, the more confused I felt about who I was. I didn't know where I fitted. I felt I was just being a machine, without a life. I needed to be able to calm down and I couldn't.

I asked my Pop for help, because he's always been around when I've needed him. Next thing, there was a job advert in the paper looking for a head chef in a boarding school, Diocesan School for Girls in Hamilton. The hours were 7 a.m. until 3 p.m., Monday to Friday. I knew this was a job that might make it possible for me to be 'normal' in the way those people I used to watch going home at night, when I was working at Nuts and Crackers, were 'normal'.

'Oh, let's get that job, got to get that job, got to get that job, got to get that job.' And I got the job, and I stayed there for two and a half years, and I progressed from head chef to catering manager. We catered for weddings and special functions, along with cooking for the boarding schoolgirls. The food was exquisite by any boarding school standard. All in all, I had really good staff and I had a pretty cruisy life.

Seriously, I'd start at seven and be finished by three o'clock and then I'd be gone. It was really smooth, and we had a really good team behind us. It was just too easy. That was the longest I'd stayed in one job.

There was complete downtime which allowed me to discover myself. I slowed down for the first time in I don't know how long – perhaps ever! Certainly since I'd been sent to boarding school.

I'd be home by two thirty, and spend time pottering around the garden or playing with Javan outside. I really felt good about life. But it was hard on us as a couple, because I'd get home, spend an hour or two with Rachael and she'd go to work in the restaurant at night, so we hardly ever saw each other. But I spent quality time with my son – cooking his dinners and having him on the hip. We used to go everywhere together, and for me that was really important.

However, the downside of this was that I just got really bored. Three months before my contract was up, the school gave me a review and said, 'Kel, what do you want to do?'

'Well,' I said, 'to be honest with you guys, I really like it but I know my time's done.' They weren't very happy about that, but I knew that what I'd said was the truth. I really stuck it out to get a good base, tried really hard to just have that money coming in constantly, but I was now bored out of my tree. I knew something was coming, I could feel it, and so I wasn't worried about giving up my contract.

'What are you going to do?' they asked.

'I don't know. That's up to whoever,' because I was starting to think like this a lot more – that something would just turn up because all these things had already been written down for me. I would think things like, 'Who am I going to meet today?' And whoever I thought about would turn up out of the blue. Those sorts of things started getting bigger and bigger.

So, the three-month contract had to be worked out, which was cool, and then one day a couple of weeks before I finished, the phone rang. A year earlier, I'd sent my CV to a hotel on a tropical island. Now, I picked up the phone.

'Yeah, gidday, I'm Duncan Jones from Vava'u, in Tonga, and I run a hotel and I got your CV and I need a chef.'

I had a talk to him and he said, 'When do you think you can get here?'

'When do you need me there?'

'Fourteen days.'

'Hang on.' I called Rachael. 'Honey! That job in the islands that I applied for a year ago, they want me there in fourteen days, what do you think?'

'Do you want to do it?' she asked.

'Do you?'

She said, 'Yeah.'

'All right,' I said. Then I was back on the phone to Duncan Jones. 'Sir, I've got a wife and a child.'

'Don't you worry, I'll fly them over here too.'

So, I finished at the school on the Friday, spent the weekend packing, and flew out on the Monday morning.

CHAPTER TWELVE

A dark spirit in our house

ALTHOUGH Rachael and I were extremely close, my increasing awareness of my gift was a side to me that I didn't tell anyone about. I suppose I was too uncertain of it to discuss it and had a feeling that I should keep it quiet. Initially, anyway, I was working so hard, and focusing on making a living for my family.

We went to Vava'u in Tonga, which lies in the South Pacific. Rachael and Javan flew over to join me about six weeks after I had arrived. It was a beautiful place. But unfortunately, the isolation sent us troppo. Then there was a cyclone, and we'd pretty much had enough after that.

One day, as we sat on the balcony of this hotel, a beautiful place, Rachael asked, 'What do you want to do?'

I opened my mouth and this weird stuff came out. 'You know, we're going to live by the lakes and then I'm going to live by the sea.'

'What?'

'We can live by the lakes, and then I'm going to live by the sea.'

'What do you mean?'

'I don't know,' I said. 'I just feel like the lakes and then the sea. It's really important.'

Eventually, we flew back to New Zealand and spent a pretty un-settled few months – we were both extremely depressed after going troppo, and then returning to everyday life in New Zealand, with nowhere to go. We stayed in Te Aroha with her mother for a few months, and then I spent some savings on a van. It was a Toyota HiAce, long base, and I made it into a little camper. We planned to do a trip around New Zealand, getting work along the way and all that sort of stuff. We went from Te Aroha to the Bay of Islands, where I got a job on the game fishing boats, because I'd had some experience in Tonga. But with me always at sea it was too hard on Rachael.

We came back down to Te Aroha, and I decided I had to get a decent job. I applied for one in Rotorua and got it, so we moved again. There were the lakes, just as I'd foretold, but I didn't click until we got there.

I began working full time as head chef in an extremely busy restaurant. We'd be doing between 200 and 300 covers a night so I was right back to working in a full-on crazy environment. I was hardly ever home and when I was home I was asleep. I had to do a split shift so during my two hours off, I'd go home and Rachael and Javan would be there but I'd just be so exhausted.

Not long after we'd moved to Rotorua, Rachael wanted to buy a house and I said, 'Well, you find a house, we'll just do it.' We were able to do that as we had a few dollars in the bank, thanks to winning the case I brought against my former employer, the one who tried to do me out of the profit-sharing deal.

She found this house and I agreed, so we bought it. Life should have been on the up then – I was working, we had our own house, things were sweet. But it just went downhill from there; it went pear shaped.

Rotorua is a very spiritual place. The lakes and hills and forest all play an amazing part in its spiritual history. Maori know a lot of spiritual things but don't always let on. I was having strong pictures come into my head when I was asleep and awake – vivid, confusing dreams that I later realised were visionary, but at the time meant nothing to me. The spirit was teaching me and it was getting stronger and stronger.

I wasn't happy at work. I'd say to the boss, 'Morning. How's it going?'

'Why the f*@k do you always say good morning? It's not a good morning.'

One day I was on the phone ordering stuff. 'Oh, hi, how's it going, it's Kelvin here from the restaurant, blah, blah, blah, we need this, this, this.'

I got off the phone and the owner's girlfriend, who was the maître d' said, 'Why the f*@k are you so nice to everyone?'

It was just always like that, and it didn't make me very happy – those sorts of conversation, or those sorts of people.

In the end, I couldn't take it anymore and had an argument with my boss. He wanted me to change the menu so I gave him three different options but nothing I suggested was ever good enough. It wasn't what he wanted, and then he and two of his waitresses came up with their own menu.

I was not only exhausted, but felt completely misunderstood and useless, just as I used to feel when I was a kid.

I said to him, 'You know, you've asked me to do the job, that's what I'm paid to do. What it comes down to is that you're trying to get me out of here.'

'That's exactly what I want,' he said. 'Get the f*@k out of my restaurant, rah, rah, rah.'

I hadn't done anything to deserve that. But I just stood up and said, 'That's it. I don't need your rubbish. Do your own cooking.'

I went home and Rachael said, 'You all right, babe?'

'Ah, we haven't got a job.'

She knew things had been getting pretty bad, and she just said, 'That's all right, we'll sort something out.' The restaurant trade has always had a high employee turnover. It's not that I didn't want to stick to a job, it's just the nature of the industry.

I sat on the couch for a week, probably, just sat there staring at the wall. While the job had been very stressful and the people nasty, I wondered whether the house had contributed to how I was feeling. It clearly had a lot of history remaining in some form, and the residue from past events can remain and cause issues in a house if it's not cleared or blessed by a kaumatua (Maori tribal elder), spiritual medium or priest. But even so, at that time I felt like a washing machine of energies, both good and bad, and I had to find my way through all that to find myself. Things were just about to come to a head.

Rachael woke up one night, screaming in fear. She felt that somebody was standing over her while she slept.

I said, 'Oh, don't be silly, just go back to sleep.' A couple of nights later she did it again, and her fear was incredibly intense. I said, 'Babe, it's okay, just tell him to go away, he'll go away.'

I didn't take it very seriously until the next time, when I sat up and saw too what Rachael had seen. It was a huge figure, probably seven foot tall, wrapped in black, and accompanied by a very offensive odour. If you stared through the black you could see what I can only describe as melting flesh with rancid eyes and long fingernails. The whole thing had a presence that turned my stomach. It was like looking at those ugly monsters on *Lord of the Rings*.

Dark energy exists and the dark side will seek you if it feels you have something that it wants.

I believe Rachael is a good person and that she was being tormented by these dark energies so that I would wake up and discover the real me. In other words, if she had not freaked out, I would probably still be working in a restaurant and maybe, just maybe, I wouldn't have opened to the possibility that spirits are real and true, that they can and do make a big difference in the world.

I choose not to have dark energy in my life. I acknowledge it, understand it and set it free with love. That night, as soon as I sat up and saw the menacing figure, thus acknowledging it, it disappeared.

'Babe,' I said. 'I've just seen what you're talking about, we've got to do something about it.' It scared me. It was obviously something really evil. 'Have you thought about asking someone from a church to come in and do something with it?'

She agreed and we spoke to our neighbours, who were Christians, and they put us in touch with their local pastor.

Javan and I were at home when the pastor and some other people from the church came along. I said to Javan, 'Are you going to come inside with us, bubba?'

I'm not going in there, Daddy, scary.'

'Okay. Fair enough.'

He stood on the verandah and refused to come into the house. That was my sign – if my boy wasn't coming in, it must be pretty serious.

The priest did his thing and when we got to our bedroom, and Rachael's side of the room, things became really intense. The priest was starting to struggle and stutter his words and began to shake, and he got quite serious about it, really intense.

At last he said, 'Oh, they've gone now, it's all good.'

But as I stood there, all I could see was that this energy was still there. 'I don't think it's gone,' I said.

He insisted that the power of Christ had got rid of that negative energy, and in the end I just agreed with him. I didn't want to step on anyone's toes; he was an elder.

But the problem didn't go away. Rachael still felt uncomfortable on recurring nights. One night it happened to her again, while I was away. The next morning my brother rang up to see how we all were, and as he was talking to Rachael, she told him about the dark energy in the house and how it hadn't been shifted by the priest. She didn't want to be in the house anymore, she told him.

Murray told her he had a friend who was a clairvoyant and that he'd bring her down. Rachael agreed.

When I got back, she told me, 'Oh, Muz is coming down on Friday with some lady to help clear the house.'

'Some lady?'

'Yeah, a clairvoyant who might be able to help us with this thing.'

'You mean a witch or something?' I asked. At that time I knew nothing about all that sort of stuff. All I knew was what I felt or saw but, being dyslexic, I'd never read any books that might have taught me more about such things.

'Well, I don't know,' Rachael said, 'but he says that she can help clear houses, and we need this house cleared because I'm not sleeping.'

'Okay, if that's what you feel is good, then do it,' I said. So, Friday came along and my brother turned up with the clairvoyant.

'Hey, bro,' he said.

'Hey, man.' I hadn't seen him for ages. Really, I was thinking, what on earth are you up to, mate, and where did you find *her*? This lady was the stereotype clairvoyant: dark hair, dark clothes, olive skin, hippy-ish. There was definitely something weird about her, and she wouldn't stop staring at me. Her name was Valerie.

I said, 'Hi, how are you?' and she just said, 'We'll do the clearing, but *you* have to leave.'

'Why? It's my home.'

But she insisted. 'No, you have to leave so that I can do the job.'

'Well, when do I come back?'

And she said, 'You'll know when to come back.'

Rachael was getting upset so we left and went down the road to a friend's place. I was really agitated, feeling really nervous and unsure. We'd been away about an hour and a half when, suddenly, I felt really calm.

'Come on,' I said to Rachael. 'I think we should go back.'

As we drove into the driveway they were just finishing. Perfect timing, I thought. We went onto the section and it felt really good. Then we went into the house and it was completely calm and peaceful – we just felt huge relief. I was really excited about it. 'How on earth did you do that?' I asked.

Valerie sat down at the table and I made her a cup of tea. She was still staring at me in that odd way, and then she said, 'Can I ask you something?'

'Yeah,' I said, looking at Rachael, thinking, what's she going to say?

She said, 'I've got a friend of yours standing here.'

'What?' I had *no* idea what she was talking about.

'Since we've cleared the house we've got a friend of yours standing here. He's got, you know, really, really hairy arms, like probably three times what you've got, this guy, and he's in his fifties. He's passed in an accident and he wants me to make sure that you know that he's okay, that he passed quickly.'

Just two weeks earlier I'd buried a friend of mine who was killed in a logging accident. We used to give him absolute grief about his hairy arms. So I knew straight away who it was.

I was completely blown away and asked her how she'd done that. She reached over and put her hands on mine. 'All you have to do is ask, and they'll be there,' she said.

And I clicked. I said to myself, hang on a second, who have I been looking at all my life? Who are the people that come and go, that no one else sees, and that make me feel I'm going crackers?

Valerie told me, 'You know you can do it too, but all you have to do is ask.'

Apparently she could tell just by looking at me.

CHAPTER THIRTEEN

Channelling negative energy

A COUPLE of days later I went trout fishing. I was sitting alone on the side of a beautiful stream, surrounded by bush, thinking about what Valerie had told me. I said to myself, if I have to ask then I'll ask my Pop. Because Pop had said to me, way back when I was just a small boy, if I ever needed him I should ask him.

I decided to test this stuff out. I said, 'Righto Pop, I'd really like five trout, but it needs to be within half an hour. So then I'll really, truly know that you're there.'

I cast my line, and I got five trout in 27 minutes. I was absolutely gobsmacked. I sat on the bank and had a little cry, thinking, wow, that is *so* cool. The only thing I hadn't done was specify how big the trout should be, and they were all little yearlings, they were all tiny. But that didn't matter, I got five within the allotted time.

It was early evening and perfect conditions – not a breath of wind, the stars starting to come out and everything was crystal clear.

I could hear the crickets; it was really cool. I sat there on the bank and I thought, wow, this is so amazing … and then suddenly a picture came into my mind, from nowhere. So I decided to follow it, to see what it meant. The image was a tandem pushbike, a guy in the front with a red jacket on, a female on the back with a yellow jacket on, a flag on the side of the road. I wondered why on earth I was getting this image, what was it all about?

I began to feel a bit frightened out there in the twilight, so decided I'd go home. I drove two kilometres up the road, turned a corner and there was a tandem bike with a guy with a red jacket on it, a lady with a yellow jacket on the back, and the flag. I literally just about ran them off the road, I was so shocked. It was exactly what I'd just seen in my head.

I stopped and pulled off the road. I thought, oh my god, that's just absolutely amazing. How does all this work? Why is this happening to me? Who am I? I was 27 and it was all starting to happen.

I got home and said to Rachael, 'Crikey, you're not going to believe what just happened.'

'What?'

I told her about the trout and the tandem bike. And she said, 'Oh, no, that can't be true.'

'Nah, but it is. It just happened.'

She was really shocked, but I carried on.

'Well, do you want me to show you what I think?'

'Sure.'

'Well, I actually think that your great-grandmother whose name is such-and-such, who I've never met but you did, is standing right here right now.'

And Rachael said, 'How do you know her name? I've never spoken of her.'

'Because she's telling me her name, she's standing here.'

Rachael wouldn't believe me and when I went on to tell her something that had happened to her as a child, she became upset.

'You're not allowed to do that! That's evil, what you're doing.'

'It can't be evil,' I said, 'because heaven's a beautiful place. That's where she's telling me she's coming from and she wants me to let you know that she's here for you.'

But Rachael was unimpressed – my revelation went down like a lead balloon. And that was the beginning of the end of us to be honest. As soon as it became personal to her, she freaked out and I can understand why – one minute she had a husband who'd quit his job, and wasn't doing that great, but those were things we could have worked through. But now I was seeing her great-grandmother, and naming her. Where had the guy she'd married gone?

I totally see her side of the story. I would have been freaked out, too. She talked to our friends about it, including a person who was a psychiatric nurse, and so then she had all these people telling her, 'He's hearing voices, he's schizophrenic, he's bi-polar, he's doing this, he's doing that.'

At the same time, I was coming under pressure from Valerie. After my experiences with the trout, and the tandem bike, and especially with Rachael's great-grandmother, I had talked to my brother, and he'd told Valerie that I obviously had some ability. Valerie began calling me, saying I needed to become involved with her spiritually, and that she needed my help with certain things she was doing.

She said, 'Look, we really want to have a meeting with you.' So, I met with her, my brother and two of his friends, Catho and Trish, and they were talking about people channelling and connecting with spirit people, and visions.

Channelling is when you allow spirit energy to come forward into your body. It steps into your body and you step out, and it talks through you. It's a bit like speaking in tongues, or a kind of possession. They used to do a lot of it in the old days. I'm quite opinionated about this sort of thing nowadays. I think it's very, very dangerous.

So there was I, brand new to all this psychic stuff, and I went into a meeting with Valerie and the others. I went into a trance and I started channelling and speaking. I didn't call for it, I didn't ask for it, it just happened. I was speaking in English, but it turned out to be, apparently, Valerie's spirit guide.

Spirit guides are energies that support us. Usually they're family members who have crossed over, or they can be angels such as Michael, Gabriel, Asrial – the list goes on. Some people believe that spirit guides can be Native Americans, Hindu gurus, Christ, Buddha, and so on. I strongly believe that we understand who our spirit guides are by asking ourselves and listening to our own heart. We already know inside ourselves; we just have to be true to ourselves and trust our instincts as to what makes our heart sing.

The thing that I don't buy is when people take a clairvoyant's word as to who guides them. I have several spirit guides who guide me with love, and I will talk about them a bit later on in this book. But it is very clear that Valerie's spirit guide was a very dark energy.

When I was channelling, I always saw really bad stuff. And just as I was about to click back into my system they'd be all light and fluffy and then I'd forget all the bad stuff. It was like a wolf in sheep's clothing. I can't remember what I was saying when I was channelling, but apparently I – or, really, her spirit guide – was talking about all these things that Valerie needed to do and release.

Valerie recognised that I had the ability to work with spirit really well – and her recognition opened the floodgates. For me, seeing spirit extremely clearly and understanding it for the first time, being able to make these connections so easily, and being recognised for it, was incredibly exciting. It was new and inspiring, and probably overwhelming – for the first time in my life I was actually set free and properly understood.

However I soon started not feeling right, feeling really heavy, and as if I wasn't a good person anymore. The excitement of this new understanding was also partly my ego causing me to be blind to the things that were not so good. My health started failing, my head was going in all directions, I didn't know who I was, and Valerie told me if I didn't help her I would get really hurt and they'd take my kid from me. She was manipulating my psyche; it was like being in the occult. It was very intense.

Even though I had only known Valerie a few months, I was so naïve, and so caught up in this new way of looking at my spirituality, that I ended up going on a couple of spiritual journeys with her that would ultimately cost me my marriage.

Lake Tarawera is important to me personally as it's where my grandfather's ashes were scattered, but it's also a very powerful and spiritual place for Maori people, with a lot of history and spiritual belief attached to it. There's a well-known story that, 11 days before the eruption of Mt Tarawera in 1886, which was to kill more than a hundred people and destroy the world-famous Pink and White Terraces, a boatload of European tourists and Maori guides saw a waka (canoe) crossing Lake Tarawera. The waka was not physically real – it was a ghost waka, a warning of the impending destruction. At that time, a Maori priest said it was a warning sign that all would be overwhelmed.

The Maori people have put a shield across the lake, keeping the dark energy at the bottom of the lake.

There are a lot of other points in New Zealand that are also very, very powerful and Valerie wanted me to release these energies. This was what her spirit guide, channelled through me, was advising her to do. She didn't have the capabilities to do it herself but she thought that I did.

Why would she want to release such powerful spiritual energies? She said that if we didn't release these energy blocks to certain parts of New Zealand then things wouldn't be right for people, and of course I got misled by that. To be really blunt, people who talk about releasing the energy of the earth are way off beam. Yes, there is earth energy, there are ley lines, there are all sorts of powerful energies, but you don't mess with them. It's the kind of dangerous stuff that ultimately ends up hurting you and the people that you care about.

Valerie's real goal was to release those energies as beacons that would bring her mothership from outer space closer to the earth.

This brings us into a very strange and dark area of spiritual energy, verging onto some very scary areas to do with extra-terrestrial beings. I want my readers to know that, while I know those sorts of things exist in the positive and the negative, I have completely excluded them from my life. I've experienced different energy forms, the dark side of things, and demonic energies. But I don't have them in my life – I have never intentionally done anything bad with my gift, and I never intend to.

In hindsight, I can say that Valerie taught me a very valuable lesson – to listen to my own heart and not to hers or anybody else's. What I see, what I hear, what I feel is mine alone.

But at that time, Valerie had convinced me and scared me into helping her, even to the detriment of my family. Neither I nor the others – my brother, Catho and Trish – knew what the hell we were doing. We were all young and naïve, and pretty much roped in. She was a very powerful, manipulative individual.

CHAPTER FOURTEEN

Calling in the spirits

I HAD a dream that I needed to carve myself a special stick to call in the spirits at Lake Tarawera. In my dream, I had to select a certain piece of wood from a certain tree – a rimu – but of course it had to be a fallen branch. All these things constitute respect. I dreamed that, and so I did that. I was guided to carve it out and I got some flax and plaited it into a rope that I attached to it.

Then Valerie, my brother and I went on a hikoi (a special ceremonial journey) over to the other side of the lake. In my 12-foot dinghy we crossed Lake Tarawera to the mountain. We landed and walked up some paths and then I found a pine-tree stump and stood on it, over-looking everything. I swung the stick around, whoo, whoo, whoo, and called all the wairua (spirits) in to help release what was in the lake.

It was absolutely amazing, just like a dream – I could see all the spirit energy coming across the land, warriors, elders, tupuna, coming from all over the place to meet.

My brother said, 'You all right, bro?'

'Mate, there's just stuff coming in from all directions.'

When they came close, the elders, there were about seven of them, said, 'We must sit and talk. The others must leave.' I told the others, 'Okay guys, you must go.'

They had a hui (a meeting or discussion), saying, 'Who's this guy here? How come he's called us in? Why should we release what's in the lake?'

My affiliation with Maoridom is quite strong, always has been since I was a kid, but the questions were starting to whisper in my mind: who was I, as a Pakeha, to intervene with those sorts of things? Who did I think I was?

On our way back across the lake, the waves were roughing up badly, and just as we got back to the boat ramp, with Valerie still in the boat, a dark shadow came up underneath the boat. I said, 'I'm out of here, this is not good.' We got back in the vehicle and headed off home. I was looking at my brother and my brother was looking at me and I said 'Mate, this is some pretty serious stuff.'

I started questioning what I was doing – if we were supposed to be doing something really positive, why was I seeing this dark stuff? Things began to click into place.

Then I remembered the story my grandfather told me, about the ghost waka that came through the fog before Mt Tarawera erupted – the warning. As we were leaving the lake I looked back down and I could see the waka coming across the lake and through the clouds, and I thought, 'Man, this is not good at all.' I was really freaking out and knew that what I'd seen wasn't good. I told Valerie and she just said, 'Oh they're there to protect us and they're there to look after us.' But she was just twisting everything around, and I knew in my heart that it wasn't right; it wasn't what I had been taught. But her position was, 'I'm the boss, and I'm the spiritual leader here and who are you to say this is bad?'

I went home and tried to calm down, and then a couple of weeks later I got a phone call from my brother saying, 'Valerie wants to talk to you.'

I went up to Hamilton to see her. 'We need to go to Kaikohe, there's another release to be done there. If you don't come I'm going to die,' she said. Looking back now I can see she was crackers and made me feel really bad, but I was also very hooked into her reality and her influence.

By this stage Rachael wasn't really speaking to me, but I needed to tell her what I was doing. That didn't go down very well. I crouched beside her side of the bed at about four in the morning telling her I had to leave to go up north with Valerie. I was so manipulated that I even told Rachael that if I didn't go, Valerie would die. I can see now how stupid that is, but at the time I really believed it.

She begged me, 'Don't go, please don't go, it's not right, it doesn't feel right for me and I'm really worried.' But I went. I went to Kaikohe with Valerie and I don't think she even knew where she was going.

We did meet some people up there, some Maori elders, and had a conversation with them about extra-terrestrials. The really weird thing is that when they started talking about it, I just went blank. I could see them talking but I couldn't hear anything; it was as if I missed the whole conversation. And things started getting weirder and weirder.

Kaikohe, and the West Coast, is spiritually incredibly powerful and lively. Apparently New Zealand's a highway for extra-terrestrial planes, and if the energy in the land can be released, it acts as a beacon to these beings to come in closer. I haven't seen any, but many claim to have seen UFOs and stuff like that up north.

This is not easy to write about because I don't want people to think that I'm a nut job, talking about this sort of stuff. But, I did go to Kaikohe with Valerie, we had a meeting in a marae, did some mahi, some spiritual work with the land. I was asked to undo the energy mass, and I did it. It's like putting a top on a bottle of pears – it's sealed in for a very good reason, to keep it from going bad. As weird as it may sound, I have the ability to be able to undo the jar spiritually. The Maori people up there were all for that sort of thing – they thought that if we put the beacons on the land, their extra-terrestrial spirit people could get closer to them. If somebody came along with the ability, then they'd allow it to happen. It's not necessarily a bad energy, but it's inappropriate to mess with it.

So, here I was thinking I was doing something really positive, but then the signs come back. We called into my mother's place in Paihia, and my Mum just listened and she said to me as I left, 'I don't feel good about her, Kel.'

'Oh no, she's wonderful, she's been really good to me,' I said.

'I don't feel good about her at all,' Mum said.

Eventually I got back to Rotorua and Rachael was really distressed and worried and I got really angry with her. 'What are you worried about?' I didn't want to admit that anything was wrong. All around me people were concerned that I was talking to dead people. My friend who was a psych nurse asked me, 'What's happening?'

'I'm seeing heaps of stuff, it's really cool,' I told her. My friend just couldn't get it at all, and I was so hyped up from recognising my own abilities that I failed to recognise that Valerie was not a good influence. I loved my wife and I loved my friends and I trusted them. I trusted them, and therefore I could talk to them, I thought. But talking about this stuff turned out to be my downfall.

Soon after, Valerie and I were in her flat in Hamilton with my brother, Trish and Catho. I was channelling again, in a total trance, and I could see myself, as if I was standing in the corner of the room watching what was going on. I went to get back into my system, into my own body, but I couldn't. The only way I can describe it is that it was like being on the edge of a bottomless well, with my fingernails clawing into the brick – that's how close I was to not being able to get back into myself. The energy of Valerie's spirit guide wouldn't allow me to step back in, and I became terrified.

I could hear Trish praying for me – I couldn't hear her physically but I could hear her spiritually, the sweet sound of this woman doing this beautiful prayer, and from my corner of the room I could *see* Trish, talking prayer to herself. I remember her saying to me, 'Fight, Kelvin, fight.'

I managed, obviously, to get back in. I was soaking in tears. I looked across the room and Trish was absolutely exhausted.

Valerie was screaming, 'Bring him back, bring him back!' I looked at her, and I said, 'What are your thoughts on Jesus?' And she just went off her nut, and spoke absolutely disgustingly of Jesus in a way that I've never heard anyone speak.

I questioned her even more about some of the things that I was seeing and why every time I channelled it would be really horrible stuff.

When you channel you speak but you don't remember what you say – I never knew afterwards what had gone on. I was translating all this stuff that needed to be done, or whatever, and then just before I came out of trance, I would see all these beautiful things, and so I would only remember the beautiful things. Years later, I now question everything I do spiritually, and know in spirit who to trust and who not to trust.

Channelling can be extremely manipulative and you have to be on your guard against such things. There's no doubt that most people will be shocked at what happened to me during that channelling, because it's really left of centre, and it was out there for me, totally. But it made me very wary, very cautious and aware of negative energies, and gave me a strong feeling that I don't want anything to do with it.

That's why I believe you must always be mindful of the negative. Have your wits about you because negative energies will trick you, take you over and get you into serious trouble within your own self.

When I do my shows, I always work very hard to validate the spirit coming through. 'I've got your dad here, he's talking about having a missing finger. Do you understand what I'm saying?' And if that person says, 'Yeah' I know that spirit's telling me the truth.

That period with Valerie also taught me the important lesson to be careful of who I hang out with. I knew then that I didn't want anything to do with such a selfish, nasty, vindictive lady, who was playing with dangerous forces that she had no right to be playing with. I no longer wanted anything to do with her, and that feeling was utterly validated by her disgusting reaction to the name of Jesus.

Jesus for me is my brother and somebody who's supported me through my entire life, from the time of my earliest memories.

I can remember when I was very small, standing out in my Nan's garden by the roses. She'd given me a little shovel and got me to make a brick edging around her roses – cleverly giving me something to do, as usual. She came outside and she was all dollied up.

'Where are you going, Nan?' I asked.

She said, 'I'm going to talk to Jesus.'

'You can talk to him out here,' I said.

'No, son, I'm going to church,' she said. 'Would you like to come?'

'No, I can talk to him here,' I replied.

I had no real, detailed idea who Jesus was at that stage, but I knew he was my friend and I could talk to him any time I wanted.

Nan had on a hat, and a brooch in her jacket, a handbag, gloves – all dressed up for Jesus. But for me, and this is quite personal of course, the creator, God, the universe is everywhere you're looking, and you are part of all of this. Going to church is fine for people who need to do that. I personally have absolutely no issues with it whatsoever – in fact, I still go every now and again. When I see my mother, I normally go to her services and that's fine.

My point is that, no matter what, even as a kid when my Nan was going to church, I knew God was everywhere, that's what I knew to be true for me. And Jesus is a huge part of that for me, so to hear Valerie abusing the name of Jesus made things very clear for me.

That episode had freaked us all out, and so the four of us – Muz, Trish, Catho and myself – knew we had to walk away from the situation. 'This isn't right,' we told Valerie. 'We can't help you any further. This journey is not ours; it's yours, and you're using us.'

It was really hard to walk away from someone who had control over us spiritually, but we had to. We gathered together the things she'd given to us, pictures or crystals, and the next day we went and put them on her doorstep.

It was only about six weeks that I was involved with Valerie, but in that time my whole life fell to bits. By this stage, Rachael was really struggling to cope with the idea that her husband was now totally deranged, talking to Jesus and hanging out with some lady who was dragging him all over the country. We had temporarily separated, and I was staying with my brother in Hamilton.

A couple of days after my final channelling with Valerie, we had a family function. Rachael and Javan came up for it, and after they left I was outside talking to Muz, when all of a sudden I couldn't breathe. I felt like I was being strangled, and I was on my knees trying to breathe and my brother was saying, 'What the hell's going on with you?'

'Someone's got me by the throat, I don't understand what's going on.' Birds in the area all went crazy, all the animals around us were screaming, dogs were barking, it was just really scary, and I couldn't breathe. It felt as if I was being spiritually attacked by a dark energy.

It was obvious to me what was happening – Valerie was very angry with us, especially with me, and wanted us to continue on with the journey of release. We'd said no, and so I was the one to cop her anger and her negative vibration – I was the one who was wide open to this stuff.

My brother was freaking out – I remember him trying to say a prayer and then he rang Catho and asked her what we should do.

'Say a prayer. He'll be fine if you keep saying a prayer,' she said. So he kept praying and I eventually came right – the darkness went away and everything went back to normal. I swear to god I thought I was going to suffocate, it was so bizarre. We rang Catho back and I spoke to her and I was crying.

'This dark energy's trying to strangle me, I don't understand, I don't know what to do about it, I'm really scared,' I said.

Then Catho, who's a real sweetheart and knew that I needed some healing after my experiences with Valerie, said to me, 'You need to come and see Aunty. I'll come pick you up.'

CHAPTER FIFTEEN

'Now, boy, you've got to make this right.'

TAURANGA is a small city on the east coast of the North Island. It's famous for its beaches – one of those places where the wide strip of white sandy beach, the deep blue of the sea and the paler blue of the sky make gorgeous stripes that you can just sit and stare at for hours. It's not that far from Hamilton and Rotorua – just over the hill. Now that it's a favourite retirement destination, it's become very built up but there are still a few of the old, fibrolite baches left from the days when it was mostly a place to spend your summer holidays.

Catho knew a lady there called Sharon whom everyone called Aunty. She's Pakeha and lives in a little, rundown old bach with her husband Jimmy, her little foxy dog and a couple of cats. She has white hair, but in between her eyes on her brow, where what we call the third eye resides, was a teardrop shape of fluorescent pink, indicating that she prayed and had visions every day. She was lovely, and she said, 'Come in, have a cup of tea and some bikkies.'

The white light coming out of her was amazing. She had a beautiful presence about her. She looked at me and said 'Come on, boy, we need to have a talk.' So we all walked in, my brother, Catho, and myself, into the lounge.

As soon as I entered that room I had the overwhelming feeling of safety. Her lounge had pictures of Jesus, positive affirmations, some nice crystals and a few books. It really was just a humble old bach. I went to sit on the couch.

'No boy, you sit here,' she said, and so I sat on my knees on the floor beside her. She sat on her chair and her third eye just started to glow.

'Oh yes,' she said, 'you've been doing things you shouldn't have, boy.'

'I'm not sure,' I said. 'I think so. I was only trying to do good things.'

'Boy, you've done some not so good things and we need to fix this.' She sat for a while quietly and then she said, 'You've been dealing with things that you're not allowed to deal with. It's somebody else's journey, not yours. It's forbidden. You must fix it. But first we must release the darkness that's with you.'

She had a crystal – an amethyst. 'You need to hold on to this,' she said, and I put my hand on it.

Crystals are used to help heal the mind, body and soul. They store and give out healing energy and can remove and retain negative energy, and after every clearing they must be cleansed with prayer and water.

'No, no, hold on to it. Put your hands out.' I took it and held it, and she put her hand out over my head and began doing a prayer over me.

I started shaking and crying. I was scared. I'd been strangled and I couldn't sleep and all this stuff was going on, and now it was like a vacuum feeling came over me. Imagine if you had a really sodden woollen coat on – and then imagine that feeling of lightness once you get it off. That was what I felt, but it came with a feeling of extreme peace as well.

However, that soon passed and was replaced with a horrible sickly feeling. I wanted to vomit, and I was very emotionally upset.

'I'm sorry, I'm sorry,' I gasped, and as I spoke, the crystal smashed in my hands. It was as if the darkness was being pulled up through my body and this crystal was channelling out all this yucky stuff. The feeling was one of enormous relief.

I looked over and my brother and Catho were both crying. It was emotionally charged because they'd seen me go through this stuff, especially when I was channelling things. Even Aunty was crying and I didn't know her from a bar of soap – she was crying and doing her prayer. It was amazing and very intense.

She took one of the broken pieces of crystal and placed it in my hand. 'This is a reminder. You don't mess with things you don't understand. You don't play games with spiritual stuff. Don't be misled by anyone ever again. Question everything and stand your ground. When it's true, stand your ground, and never let anyone walk on you. You've learnt your lesson the hardest way possible.'

I still have that piece of crystal to remind me of how Aunty released darkness from me, and all that I learnt that day. She said, 'If you put your mind to the good energy, you can help people who need the help. This is what your goal is to be.' Aunty changed my life there and then.

In order for me to see her power and ability, she gave me a reading that completely blew me away. She told me all sorts of things about myself – the number on my letterbox, the fact that I have a son, what I had in my shed, what my car looked like. She knew things about me that even I didn't know. She was really positive with it.

She said to me, 'And your Pop loves you.' Pop had been pushed away by Valerie's spirit people, and I had lost my contact with him.

But now he was back with me.

It was such an incredible reading. It was all the things that I'd always thought that I could do – all the skills that I had been putting into negative energy.

Then she looked at me and she said, 'Now, boy, you've got to make this right. You'll know what to do, but you've got to go back and ask the spirit world for forgiveness and seal the negative energies back in place. It was sealed for a reason.'

Afterwards, I questioned Catho about what she'd told Aunty about me.

'I told her you were in trouble, that was it, nothing more, nothing less,' she said.

Aunty's an amazing woman. I went to see her about a year later and she said, 'Come in, boy, you're doing very well.'

'Yeah, I am, thanks.'

Then she said, 'Where's my Rheineck?'

I had a box of Rheineck beer for her because Catho had told me she was quite partial to it. I'd purposely left it in the car, and the old girl knew – she knew I had a box of beer in the car.

After leaving her that first time I went straight back to Tarawera. I did my prayers that Aunty had taught me, and then I got into my dinghy and went across the lake and it was completely calm. I knew that if it got rough halfway across it would mean the spirits didn't want to see me. I went up the hillside to that same tree stump, still doing my prayers, and the presence was peaceful.

I didn't need to call the wairua this time, though, because they were there waiting for me. I sat on the stump, asked them to forgive me for the things I'd done that I shouldn't have done, and asked if it would be okay if I could return in the future.

I could hear in the distance a kuia, a spirit wailing loudly, and she was getting louder and louder and as she was wailing others were dispersing, and I understood that they were dispersing because I was no longer a danger. When I'd originally called them in I thought I was calling them in to release the lake's deep energy, but really they were being called to protect what was in the lake and stop me from doing it. That's why I couldn't go any further on the day.

It's serious stuff – they are the keepers of the land, and weren't there to hurt me, but to protect me more than anything. I go to Tarawera now and the first thing I do is my prayers. When I drive into Rotorua I can see the mountain and I say, 'Hi Pop, kia ora!' I feel completely safe there, completely fine.

After making things right at Tarawera I returned to Kaikohe to the marae where I'd been before. I didn't go in because I wasn't with anyone, but everything seemed normal, everything seemed to be fine. I asked for forgiveness, and as I was doing my karakia (prayer) a twin rainbow came over the top of the marae. In Maoridom the twin rainbow symbolises forgiveness and a blessing of the wairua – it was their way of saying, 'It's okay, mate.'

After all this was done I returned home to Rotorua, where it was pretty obvious that my marriage was off the rails.

While going through all the dark spiritual stuff, dealing with Valerie and meeting Aunty, I'd also hurt my wife, my son, my friends. I couldn't see a way forward, and so when I went home to our house I decided that I'd take myself out. My state of mind was such that I felt that death would bring me enlightenment, and would be nothing but a relief to all who knew me. I had a firearms cabinet with lots of guns in it. So I took my Mauser 6.5 mm, which would seriously have blown my head off, and I loaded it and I put it in my mouth and was about to squeeze the trigger. I had reached the hard point when an angel appeared in front of me, and she said, 'What about your son?'

So I'm still here.

That was my guardian angel, and she's been with me ever since. Her name is Margaret and she is the most beautiful person I've ever seen: she has blue eyes, the longest, purest blonde hair and the most spectacular wings. She appeared so clearly, surrounded by an incredible white light. It was so bright yet it did not blind my eyes at all. I have seen her only once, but I feel her presence often, and she has since given me lots of useful information about the spirit world.

The angel from the white light loved me and I felt wanted and needed and understood.

That happened in our house, and I told Rachael about it and she asked me to leave.

I asked her to give me a couple of weeks on my own. I thought I'd head over to Tauranga looking for work, and try to sort myself out. I told her, 'You know, it doesn't have to be this way. I just can't stop what I'm seeing.'

I packed up some things and Javan came running out – he was only four – saying, 'Dad, Dad, you forgot this,' and I looked down. 'Here's your deer caller, Dad!' He looked up at me and said, 'I love you dad, it's going to be all right.' He didn't know it, but my life was in turmoil. I didn't know who I was, whether I was coming or going. Something inside me said, 'Do not come back.' So I left and I went up to the hills and hung out for a few days and cried and cried. I visited my friend Trish in Waihi for a few days. Meanwhile, Rachael moved a friend into the house to help pay the rent, which was fair enough.

About three weeks later, it was Javan's fifth birthday. I rang my brother and said, 'Mate, I really want to see my baby for his birthday, but I'm too scared to go home, they're all judging me for being different.' Muz rang Rachael and said, 'I'm bringing Kelvin over, he wants to see his boy for his birthday. Have you got any problems with that?' and she said, 'No worries.'

So my brother picked me up and took me home but I wouldn't go into the house. It was really hard. I sat on the lawn and played with Javan – and then a six foot four policeman walked through the gate.

'Are you Kelvin?'

'Yeah.'

'I want to talk to you.'

The cop and his partner walked me off the property and stood me against the cop car and said, 'Right, Kelvin, what's going on?'

'What do you mean what's going on? It's my son's birthday and I've come to see my son.'

'Apparently you've had a few problems with your firearms.'

'Nah, they're in the shed, I haven't been home, I haven't been here, I haven't got any firearms on me. They're in the shed.'

'Actually,' the big cop said, 'we have them all down the station.'

It turned out they'd taken all the firearms out of the house after Rachael had reported the fact that I'd tried to top myself.

Fair's fair, I could see why they'd done that. They felt they needed to check up on me, whether I was safe.

'Are you doing all right in your head?' they asked.

'Yeah,' I said, 'I am now. I wasn't a few weeks ago. Yeah, I'm doing okay.' We just talked and I said that if they had the guns that was fine.

'I'll give you some advice,' the big cop said. 'Don't come back to your property. They don't want you here. We've got the firearms and we're going to hold those until you've been assessed by the Fire Arms Department. Other than that you seem okay to me. Might pay to say goodbye to your boy and leave.'

After they'd gone, I got in Muz's car and we drove off and I just lost it. To turn up at your son's birthday and the police turn up and ask you to leave? It was more than I could handle. I was upset and incredibly angry and got into my van and just vanished. I disappeared, didn't see my son for three months, I missed his first day at school because I was away. The things you miss.

CHAPTER SIXTEEN

'It's time to wake up, Kelvin!'

I PARKED my van up in the hills behind Waihi – it's rugged, wild country up there, rough, craggy farmland that turns to thick dark bush on the hillsides. There's a track that runs for miles through those ranges, and it's easy to be completely isolated. I just needed to spend time with myself – a lifetime of running had to stop.

I basically had a breakdown, I think – hit a wall. I was still 27. I spent days on end sitting alone in my van, questioning the things that constituted my life, thinking and meditating. I had some nice CDs that somebody had given me, some whale music or birds chirping, and that made me feel very peaceful.

My big issue was that I was trying to differentiate between the spirit talk in my head and what was expected of me in my everyday life. It all came down to one big question: who am I? I had thought I was a chef but now I was seeing all these spirits really clearly. I knew I was different, I had always known that, but now the floodgates had opened.

I had my Bible with me, and I was trying to understand why there are so many differences of opinion within Christianity about spirituality. For instance, my wife's family are full-on churchgoers and didn't approve of the things that I was seeing, and yet Jesus Christ is hugely important to me. Why was it that just because I could see people who have died, I was seen by some as a demonic person or monster?

I was really confused because I couldn't understand why, if somebody goes to heaven, you couldn't talk to them? When they die do they turn into monsters? No they don't.

What had I done that was so wrong? Why did everyone now hate me? I didn't want to hurt anyone.

Yes, I became involved with a woman who was absolutely nuts. Valerie was probably mentally unwell, but once I recognised that and realised what was going on, I acknowledged it, knew that it wasn't for the good of people, it was for the good of one person, and then stood away from it.

I learnt the hard way and it cost me my family – I put them on hold to do something for someone else. That's why when I go to seminars and share the knowledge now, I say, 'You do not have to go to the gutter. If you explain too much to your partner straight off they may turn their backs on you because they'll be freaking out. Gently get them to come with you. Don't just blurt it out because you'll end up in the gutter and we don't want that. Marriage is marriage. That's it for life. People change and they evolve, but sometimes one of you will change more rapidly than the other, and the other one may not be ready to hear all these things so be careful how you speak at first. Gently work your way into it because they may turn on you simply because they're frightened.'

I share that as a really important message to people.

One afternoon I was sitting in the van, just thinking, and working through stuff in my head, when the whole energy in the van changed and I felt sick, uncomfortable and very frightened. I couldn't see anything but I knew something had changed in the room. I looked up and spoke. 'Who are you and what do you want?'

Nothing happened immediately, but I got this overwhelming feeling that it wasn't a good presence. I repeated, 'Who are you? What do you want?'

Suddenly, my Bible, which was sitting up on the shelf, went flying across to the other wall and fell – doof! – onto the floor.

Obviously this was a bad energy, and over the next five or six hours I learnt how to fight it. It was spiritual warfare, and that's where I learnt to do my full karakia, or prayer, until everything went back to being smooth and calm, until I was powerful or strong enough to stand my ground against it. I just stood there, saying the Lord's Prayer over and over again to release whatever it was.

That experience taught me a lot about the duality that lives inside everyone, including me. If you can imagine everyone has inside them both good and evil, positive and negative, the negative will want to stop you doing good things and the positive will support you. But you must learn what the negative feels like so that you can fight it and can use your abilities and gifts for a positive journey. You must know the opposite to yourself.

I know my good self and I know my not-so-good self. If I took that not-so-good self into real life, it would be my downfall. I could use my powers for self-gain, for Lotto numbers, and that's just not where I'm at. That would be corruption, and it's not how it's supposed to work. So, you've got to recognise the difference between positive and negative, especially with such powerful energies coming into the room.

I don't want negativity in my life, but how you deal with the presence of negative energy is very important. You must use prayers, not force. Often when people feel negative energy in the room they'll get angry and uncomfortable, telling it to go away – but that's what the negative energy wants.

I've learnt to send them away by saying: 'I acknowledge you, I feel your presence in the room, I accept you for who you are, but I choose not to have you in my life. I ask you to leave.'

If they don't leave then I ask the angels for some help: 'Hey guys, I need some help, this negative energy won't leave my presence.' And it's gone, just like that. It's not hard to understand, but I had to work it all out. I hadn't read any spiritual books because of my dyslexia, so I had to learn by sitting, talking, communicating and asking.

Margaret changed my life because she taught me more about myself than anybody. When I was doing the van thing she gave me heaps of information about the spirit world, and kept me safe. She taught me that if you don't ask you don't receive. I'd ask things such as, 'How does it work? Why me? What do I need to do? You'd better show me what you want me to do.'

I was also shown an absolutely massive story – the story of my own life that I hadn't been able to see previously. Now, thanks to the help I was getting, I was piecing all those things together and realising that they'd been trying to talk to me for ages. All the times I thought I was just imagining things when I was a kid, of knowing what was going to happen, of knowing I was going to marry Rachael, for instance – finally, I could see them for what they were. Spirit had been there all along, talking to me, showing me things.

I was taken through the corridors that I'd already seen previously when I was 21 – when I had the vision of the pathway up to heaven – and I clicked at last. 'Oh,' I realised, 'you tried to show this to me when I was 21 and I wasn't listening, I wasn't ready.' I saw things that I'd seen as a child and again I realised, 'Oh no, I've missed the boat there too.'

The answers had always been there, I just didn't have my eyes open. Now, the angels opened me up in such a way that I had no choice. 'It's time to wake up, Kelvin. Wake up!' And so I did.

It was almost as if I had been taken away from everyone to

download incredible amounts of information – where you go when you die, what happens when you get spiritually lost. All the stuff that I know I've seen with my own eyes spiritually.

The best way I can explain is like this: imagine it's a peaceful day, but the neighbour is mowing his back yard. Instead of being angry and agitated by the noise I understand that it's part of what's going on and there isn't anything I can do about it. Instead of fighting against the fact that it's a lawnmower, I tune into its vibration and sense that the vibrational tone, the humming, of the lawnmower is quite a tranquil sensation. And I can set aside all my busy, angry thoughts.

It's about trying to understand that everything happens for a reason, whether we get it right away or wait for the answers. They do work out. That was something I had to learn quite quickly.

I have another guide, another spirit man who's Aboriginal. His name's Neshka and he is a healer. His presence came to me from the white light when I was meditating, and he said to follow him. So I went for a walkabout with him and he sat me down by a fire and taught me about medicines and healing so that when I look at people I can understand roughly what's wrong with them or get the sensation that perhaps they have too much sugar in their system, high blood pressure, a broken arm when they were 12, whatever.

While I lived in the van I had many visitors from the white light. They're all good, positive people, certainly not demonic forces or energies or anyone trying to outdo anyone else. I had so many conversations – I was still connecting with Jesus and I had my Pop coming in and out again as well to make sure I was all right.

I had to experience what it was like to feel lonely – I missed my wife, I missed my son, it was incredibly painful. I spent about three months on my own in that way. Towards the end, I visited my friend Trish, a clairvoyant and a very important mentor. Then I ended up in a camping ground at Waihi because I needed a shower. And that's where the police tracked me down.

CHAPTER SEVENTEEN

'Yeah mate, I'm seeing dead people.'

THE WAIHI police had been contacted by the Rotorua police who wanted to talk to me about my firearms, which of course they still had. They also wanted me to contact my family and let them know where I was.

They said, 'Mate, you're obviously okay, but people need to know where you are.'

I didn't do it, but the police must've contacted Rachael because soon after that she turned up in the caravan park with Javan and said she wanted me to go back. The deal was I had to do two things: not live at home in my own house, so move down the road somewhere; and have psychiatric treatment.

I agreed. I had a friend called Sally who lived just one kilometre down the road from our house, and she'd always said she'd help me out if I needed anything. I made a quick phone call to her, and she said I could stay in her spare room, so I shot back to Rotorua like lightning.

So there I was, staying at Sally's, trying to work through things with Rachael and, best of all, I was seeing my boy again.

One night, though, I was feeling a little lost and worried and full of questions about what was going to happen to me. I fell asleep, but woke up after an hour or so to an incredibly bright white light in my room. I pulled back the blinds thinking maybe there was a car outside my window parked with its lights on full, but there was nothing.

I then realised that the light was coming from the wall and ceiling. As I started to focus I saw my Pop walking towards me. He had at his side a few of his hunting dogs and he smiled and told me what was going to happen to me, and he spoke of faith. 'Trust unto the light and be brave. It is through experience that we learn,' he said. 'I'm always at your side to help. Be strong my boy, as the lesson you have chosen is going to be long and hard but you will make it through and the outcome will be beyond your wildest dreams.'

And with that he turned, whistled at his dogs and walked back into the light. As he walked away the light went back to darkness and the wall and ceiling vanished into the dark of the night.

The second part of the deal with Rachael meant seeking psychiatric help, so I went to a psych doctor, and he said, 'What's happening?'

'Mate, I've been seeing dead people. No drama!'

He looked over his glasses and said, 'Seeing dead people?'

'Yeah mate, seeing dead people.'

'How's that?' he asked, with a big frown on his face.

'Well, the only way I can explain it is I'll show you.'

'Go on.'

'Well, your Dad's here, his name's Edward and he passed of a heart attack and he's telling me you're a diabetic and you're not doing your medication properly.'

He seemed very shocked. 'How do you know that?'

'Because your Dad's standing here, mate.'

124

'He can't be, he's dead.'

'That's what I'm telling you! You asked me what's going on and I'm telling you. Here comes your Mum.'

'No way.' He was tripping out. Then another doctor, a woman, came in, and he excused himself and left as quickly as he could.

The lady said, 'Hi, Kelvin.'

'Kia ora.'

'So what's happening with you?'

But by this stage I was becoming quite nervy and starting to shake. 'Well, a lot of things but I don't think I should talk anymore.'

'I think you've just spun out Dr Smith, and I think we need to talk about it,' she said.

'Well,' I told her, 'I'm seeing dead people and I'm obviously freaking people out, and I don't mean to, but it's what's happening.'

'Seeing dead people?' she asked.

So I said, 'Let's put it this way, your Mum's Mum has passed into spirit and tells me you're going on a plane on Friday and you're really scared of flying. Are you going to Dunedin?'

She just stared at me. 'No way.'

'What do you mean no way?' I asked.

'I'm flying to Dunedin on Friday.'

'Oh,' I said, 'you'll be absolutely fine, don't worry about it.' Bad move! She didn't even go. She cancelled her flights because she was so petrified of flying, and was so freaked out by this guy who was in her psych ward telling her 'you're going on a plane to Dunedin and you're going to be safe because your Nana's telling me'.

I met a few other doctors, five altogether. I didn't know who they were exactly, but the meetings were all in the same sort of vein. It must've been mayhem for them.

Anyway, Dr Smith decided that I needed medication. 'We think that you're ADHD and we need to get you to calm down because you're too hyperactive.'

I've always been hypo – I'm here to live, I'm not here to muck around. They obviously couldn't label what was going on for me.

'We're going to put you on drugs,' he said.

'Mate, I'm not a druggie, I don't want to do any drugs, I'm all right,' I said.

'It's either drugs or we're going to lock you up.'

'Okay, so I obviously don't have much of a choice?'

'No you don't. We have to put you on medication, otherwise you'll need a little bit of a spell to work out what's going on for you. As far as I can see you want your family back and so you'd be advised to do that.'

I agreed because I did want my family back. So I started taking Ritalin, which is a synthetic-based drug used primarily to treat people with ADHD. It just about killed me.

I think I spent the first week feeling like a zombie. When I rang the doctor and said, 'I don't feel very good. They're making me feel really horrible.'

'It's part of the process,' was all he'd say.

Remember, they were going to lock me up if I didn't take these things. I didn't want to be put inside some padded cell as if I was a fruit loop because I'm not. I'm a normal guy – I just see dead people.

The first couple of weeks were extremely weird. I'd become really numb. Somewhere in there my relationship with Rachael broke up for the final time, and I found all my stuff on the side of the road. She just got it all and threw it out and that was that.

I had to remain on the drugs because I was still scared about what they would do to me if I stopped. They knew when I was taking my pills. Anyway, I had to – within six weeks I was a drug addict. My body needed the synthetic-based chemicals – 80 milligrams a day was what I'd been prescribed. That's a lot of pills, but if I didn't take them, look out. If I drove an hour in one direction and realised I'd left them behind, I'd turn around to get them. I never wanted that. I never wanted to be an addict, but I knew that if I didn't take them I'd be a real mess.

I stayed on with Sal and got a couple of jobs – building stages and then as a labourer on a building site. I rented a beautiful little one-bedroom apartment right beside Lake Rotorua. It was really cool. I used to sit by the lake and just chill out.

I spent a lot of time inside myself when starting on the medication, just trying to get used to it. The spirits had became fuzzy but I worked so hard on focusing on them that I could still connect. I had constant headaches, a dry mouth all the time. I felt terrible – but I was fit, I could beat it. I was fighting it. They could put me on drugs, but they couldn't stop me from seeing dead people.

On the building site I met a really nice dude called Steve. He was Pakeha, covered in tattoos and an ex-drug addict. But now he was a born-again Christian, right into his Bible, and he and I had fantastic conversations about life and death and God and stuff, as you do, on the building site. He had a wife, Pat, and a couple of kids – absolutely beautiful people, they looked after me, and we just got on like a house on fire.

I was starting to do readings for people – word spreads quickly if you can see spirit clearly. So there would be knocks on my door.

'We've heard you can help.'

'Oh, okay.' I'd do them for nothing.

I met a couple of Maori ladies – can't remember how – Carol and Sharon, and they invited me round to their place for some kai, a feed. They were really spiritual people and we just sat and talked. They were in their fifties probably, just nice people, and it was cool making some new friends.

Carol told me that on Sundays they went to a spiritualist church, and she invited me to come with them. After much thought I decided to go.

When I walked in, I saw Carol and Sharon down the back of the room, and I waved at them. A Maori guy sitting in front of them was waving back at me and saying, 'Kia ora' because he thought I was waving at him. I just said, 'Gidday, mate' as I walked past him.

When I sat down beside Carol and Sharon, this guy turned around and said to them, 'Oh, do you know him?'

'Yeah, this is Kelvin, this is Eddie.' I thought he was a bit odd, obviously gay, and sweet as. He was in his ugg boots and a big woolly jacket.

The proceedings got underway. It was my first time in a spiritualist church, but the format was pretty standard. These churches are open to everybody. The Rotorua one was only a little group – some nights there'd be five people and some nights there'd be 50.

They met once a week. You put in your koha, your donation, whether it was $2, or if you didn't have any money some biscuits, it didn't really matter.

Then the president, or someone who was a speaker for the committee, got up and welcomed everyone, and then they went into a prayer. This could be to God, although the New Age way is to ask the universe for guidance and direction.

They'd sing a song, do an address and then sing another song and then they'd have a guest speaker. There were different guest speakers every week; people such as a Reiki master, or a medium. After that, they might do another song and then some readings, karakia, closing and that was it.

It's pretty straightforward. Some people who come along to the spiritualist centres have gifts and some people don't, but they come along to learn.

Anyway, it was at my first meeting at the Rotorua spiritualist church that I met Eddie, also known as the famous Uncle Tata. This guy changed my life. He's 60-something, the nicest, funniest old man you'll ever meet in your life.

At the end of the service we had a cup of tea and he came over to talk. There was an instant rapport, an instant connection, and we hit it off.

A week or so later I went back and they were all there again. Some of the group were meeting for dinner and they invited me along. We did some karakia (prayers) for our food and opened up the house for messages. It was nice and friendly, everyone just talking about spiritual things. They could all see spirit – they were all of a like mind. Some would do mahi, or spiritual mahi – mahi means work, so hands-on mahi is healing; some could see spirit, some could hear spirit. It was really cool.

These were obviously people I'd never met before, and so I sat there very quietly. Then the elder who was leading the meeting said to me, 'What do *you* get?'

'Pardon?' I wasn't sure what he meant.

'What do you get out of all this?'

Well, I just went around all the people and read for them which was very cool. It was just me saying, 'This is what I get, I'm in my element.' I was accepted.

It wasn't long before I wanted to speak at the centre myself. I told this same group of people that I really wanted to speak but they said I was too young and not at the right level.

'What level do you think I'm at?'

'You're just too young.'

Maybe three months had gone by when I asked them again, 'Please give me one shot and if it doesn't work I'll never do it again, please, please, please.' When somebody cancelled, the leaders agreed to give me a crack at it. Spiritualist churches are usually run for an hour, or an hour and a bit. Three hours later they didn't want me to leave. Obviously, I was doing really well, and people did not want me to stop.

THE BUZZ from doing readings for people and attending the spiritual-ist scene was one thing, but I still had to earn a living. During this time I was working on the building site and working exceptionally hard. My body was in good shape, apart from the drugs, and I was working from 7 a.m. to 6 p.m. That sort of work, hard labour, makes you ache, unable to move. I did that for a while and then I thought I'd go back to cheffing. There was a new restaurant opening up and so I applied for the job and got it. I also moved houses, as I thought spirit was telling me that was a good thing, but it all went downhill from there for a while, and I learned never to listen to spirit when you don't know who they are. If it's not your dad or your mum or someone that you really trust, and you can verify that it really is them, then you shouldn't do it. That's something that I learned the hard way again.

The restaurant I was working at was really boring – the owner's concept was not much more than just a bar. Then, about that time, Rachael moved up to Auckland to be with a new partner and took Javan with her. That was hard, so I bailed to Tauranga.

CHAPTER EIGHTEEN

From pain into the light

I WAS getting sicker and sicker with the drugs but I got myself to Tauranga and moved in with a girlfriend I'd met along the way, Patria. I was beginning to shake really badly, I couldn't breathe properly, couldn't feel anything, couldn't make love, couldn't sleep properly. I couldn't tell when I needed to go to the toilet. I couldn't digest anything, and I lost weight. On the day I drove away without my drugs and raced back to get them, that's the day I realised, 'Hang on a second, something's not right. This shouldn't be happening. I'm *wanting* my pills.'

I was missing Javan like crazy. I was only working part-time, but I'd save all my money for petrol to drive to Auckland to see my son for an hour – I had to be supervised – and drive back. That's 500 kilometres in total, there and back. Three hours each way.

It must have been really hard for Patria. She was a lovely girl, but I ended up locking myself in my room for days on end without coming out. It was terrible. I wasn't bad to her or anything like that, but I was just inside myself. I'd pray constantly to not feel that way, and pray not to have this yucky feeling come over me, and I'd ask for my body to be cleared out, but I wasn't strong enough to fight what was going wrong with my body.

One night I woke up shaking. Patria put her hands on my chest and did a nice little prayer but the shaking just got worse and I started foaming at the mouth and my neck was twisting around in spasms and my eyes were rolling backwards. I was unable to breathe and panicking, and the next thing I was on the floor convulsing.

I do not know how Patria got me in the car – she's only little – but she managed to wedge me in somehow, at the same time as she was screaming at me, trying to keep me awake.

'It's okay mate, you're going to be fine, stay with me, stay with me...' I could hear and feel her stress, feel it so crystal clear. I remember arriving at Tauranga Hospital and being pulled out of the car by the technical team and I heard them asking her what drugs I'd taken.

'He doesn't do drugs but he's on medication.'

They asked what it was and at that moment, I passed out. The lights went out. Everything went peaceful, quiet, and totally calm.

When I woke up I was strapped into a gurney. All hell had broken loose – people were injecting things into me. Patria was sitting there sobbing quietly to herself. I opened my eyes and I asked, 'Are you okay, mate?'

'Oh my god, you're all right!' and she burst into tears. I said to her, 'What happened? I don't remember.'

She told me the doctors all thought I was a drug addict OD-ing, or that I'd taken something else on top of the Ritalin. They certainly wouldn't accept there was anything wrong with the Ritalin. In the end they sent me home. They seemed to think I was all right.

That experience was what had happened in a purely physical way.

However, from the spiritual dimension, there was a lot more going on. While I was in the back of Patria's car being driven to the hospital, all I can remember is seeing crosses, a grey vision of crosses, and everything being really quiet.

I remember being pulled out of the car by somebody, and them yelling at me, but then it all went dark. Spiritually I felt myself leave my body, and I was floating in this complete darkness, this nothingness.

I experienced my feet hitting a browny-grey powder and I thought, 'What am I doing here?' It felt like the bottom of the ocean, nice sand but it was grey and everything was dark around me.

I recalled Aunty saying to me, 'No matter where you are and what you do, you always find the light, you always look for it and you go towards it.' I was looking for it. I knew something clearly wasn't right so I was looking for it and then I saw this wee speck of light amongst the darkness and I thought, 'Right, I'll get to that.'

I tried to crawl my way to it and I imagine it was how walking on the moon would be. It was that sort of heavy weightlessness, and I could only move with the greatest of effort. And then hands came out of the grey sand and were trying to hold me back, grabbing my legs, and I was panicking to get away from them. I kept telling myself to go to the light, go to the light.

These things kept grabbing my feet but I managed to break free and I started getting to this light – it was so hard, it was like swimming through something really thick.

The light got bigger, going from a pin-head to a larger circle of light; then from round to square – and when I got to the square light I woke up in the gurney in the foyer of the Tauranga Hospital.

Spiritually, I figured that what I had experienced was what it would be like if you were OD-ing on something and weren't in a good frame of mind and your transition was very difficult as a result. That's why we talk about people being lost if they suicide while on drugs.

When I left hospital I was taken back to Patria's and it took me about two weeks to get better. I felt as if I'd been hit by a bus, literally, and suffered from cramps and convulsions. My eyes were red from all the popped blood vessels. I was aching everywhere. But I was still taking the Ritalin. I had to, I was too scared not to.

At the end of that fortnight there was a spiritual gathering in Waihi Beach. My mate Eddie drove from Rotorua to Tauranga to pick me up, and with a group of friends we all went over there to stay. I had Javan with me that weekend which was really cool. Things had improved and he was allowed to stay for weekends.

At Waihi I was trying to do readings, which I shouldn't have really been doing because I wasn't so well, but I wanted to because that's what I liked to do. I was doing them for koha, so I wasn't charging anything. If you wanted to leave $5 that was cool, if you wanted to leave nothing I didn't care, it didn't matter. Yet I used to make more money than anybody else. Funny how it works.

I did one day there and it was fine, but by the Saturday night I wasn't feeling so good and by Sunday morning I was sick again – I couldn't breathe and had a sore chest. I asked Eddie to mind Javan for me while I went to the chemist down the road in Waihi.

I knew the lady who worked in the chemist – she was a friend of my family's from Huntly when I was a kid, Trisha Bailey. Trisha took one look at me and said, 'I think we might want you to sit down.'

'Okay.' And I just crashed out, taking a couple of things off the shelf with me. It was all a bit of a mess.

Trisha rang the doctor who came and put me on oxygen straight away because I wasn't breathing at all. That calmed me down somewhat, and then they tried to transport me to the medical centre and I hardly remember a thing.

At some point I came to and Eddie was standing over me crying. His glasses were fogged up, and he was saying 'Come on buddy, breathe'.

Then there was a guy in a funny-looking suit and he had my toe and he was squeezing it and yelling at me, 'Mate, hey mate, mate.' I sort of had my eyes semi-open and I could see just him across there. 'What's the problem?' and then I blanked out. Next thing I knew, I woke up in a hospital.

It turned out that when they took me to the medical centre in Waihi they'd called a helicopter to take me to Tauranga hospital. The guy grabbing my toe had been the helicopter paramedic. I don't remember a thing, except seeing the water and thinking I was having a cool dream.

Javan turned up at the hospital with Eddie, because they had to drive. While Eddie was packing up, Javan had taken some of my crystals and sold seven of them for $1 each and he'd bought a chain with a paua cross on it. When I woke up he gave it to me and he said, 'Daddy, this is for you.'

But, despite the fact I hadn't been able to breathe, the doctors there still couldn't find anything wrong with me and sent me home again. I decided the pills were killing me because I kept flat-lining, having seizures to the point of foaming at the mouth, bleeding eyes and horrendous cramps. Spiritually I was looking at it as negative energies attacking me and the message I kept getting from my angel was 'white powder, stop the white powder'. I decided to go cold turkey.

I split up with Patria. I needed to be near my son as being away from him so much was contributing to my stress levels. Eddie had moved to Auckland by that stage. He said, 'If you want to come up to Auckland, I've got a room. I want to look after you.'

So I moved to Auckland, and I got worse. There were more convulsions, bleeding eyes and vomiting and not being able to go to the toilet.

We were pretty poor and it must have been a struggle for Eddie. I was on a sickness benefit, and we were living out of the chilly bin – we didn't even have a fridge.

Imagine getting to the stage where you want to go to the toilet but you can't get out of your bed. I remember when I got the confidence to go to the toilet. Eddie was at work and I tried to get out of bed but I slid down the wall and stayed there for the whole day because I couldn't move. I was paralysed from detoxifying from the drugs. I didn't even know who Javan was.

'Who are you?' I asked him. 'You were a little kid when I saw you last, you've all grown up.' What on earth had happened to me? It was really, really hard.

After the first week or so of being up in Auckland and going cold turkey, I was feeling really bad, hallucinating, constantly shaking, and unable to go to the toilet. I said to Eddie, 'Mate, I'm not feeling so good today, I'm having a really bad day.'

'Come over here, buddy,' said Eddie. So I sat on the floor and he started rubbing my shoulders because I was so sore from cramps.

I said to him, 'Mate, it feels like something's crawling inside my body.' I pulled up my shirt and there was a mass, half the size of a tennis ball, which I believe was the accumulated toxins from the drugs – and it was moving. It was a physical thing; it wasn't a spiritual energy, and every time he went to massage it, it would shoot to somewhere else and cramp me out. It sounds weird but that's what was happening. When it got to my lungs that was when I couldn't breathe.

That same night, I had a really bad seizure. I ended up on the floor and I was in absolute agony. I'd never done this in my life but I remember whispering to Eddie, 'I want my Mum.'

Eddie rang the ambulance, and while he was waiting for it, rang Mum in the Bay of Islands and told her that I was really sick and asking for her. She was still on the phone when the ambulance guys turned up. I can remember pieces of this. 'What's wrong with you?' one of them asked, but I couldn't speak and he started screaming at me.

Eddie started saying, 'Hey, mate, just ease up. He's been on Ritalin, and he's coming off the drug.' Instantly the guy said, 'He's taken something else.'

I couldn't speak. They put an oxygen mask on me and the guy was saying, 'Sit up, sit up,' and started harassing me, abusing me. 'You can't even talk to me, you're just a druggie.' Of course, a big argument erupted between Eddie and the ambulance staff and my mother was on the phone, listening to it all. And then they left me there on the floor.

They checked my signs and stuff, but in the end they just insisted I must've taken something else, and they left.

At about 8 o'clock the next morning, Mum arrived, having driven down from the Bay of Islands. I was on the couch – I still hadn't made it out of the lounge – sitting there shaking and staring at the wall. She walked in and said, 'Are you all right, Kel?'

'Does it look like I'm all right?'

'I think we should take you to the hospital to get you checked,' she said. So she rang Eddie at work.

'Can you come home? I think I need a bit of a hand to get him in the car.'

I remember being carried into the hospital by Eddie and Mum, and I remember Mum talking to my brother on the phone and saying, 'Muz, I've got Kelvin. I've taken him to the hospital. He's not good.'

I really wasn't right. Nothing seemed to work, I couldn't get co-ordinated, I couldn't do anything. I was really messed up. I was sitting leaning forward over my knees when I said, 'Mum?'

'Yeah, Kel?' She was still talking to my brother.

'I'm going home. I love you.' And I fell forward and hit her thigh with my head and I leant into her. 'Oh no!' said Mum, 'It's okay, son, call out to Jesus, he'll help you.'

I could hear Mum screaming as I was going to the floor. I don't remember hitting the floor – I could see it coming but I couldn't do anything about it. My Pop was there, and my mates. Then that silence again but I just felt surrounded by total love, it was unreal. I can't describe the peace that I felt, the calm, the serenity, especially after having been through all the trauma. Being in such a beautiful place after being in so much pain was phenomenal, a huge release. It was completely white light. If you describe love in the fullest sense of the word, I was surrounded by it. I was ready for that.

I had conversations with two people – firstly my Pop told me a lot of personal things about what to do and how to make things better. He said I had to heal myself – so I did, and here I am now, drug-free and not ADHD or nuts.

Secondly I spoke to Jesus. He told me that my journey was to help people understand life after death, to educate folks to understand and to set them free from fear. He said that the media was the answer to it.

I now work in TV, radio and write columns for magazines in New Zealand and Australia. So I reckon Jesus has had a hand in all that.

Some of the things mentioned in those conversations have yet to be fulfilled.

I can't say whether they proved me clinically dead or not, but they worked hard to get me back. It's not every day you get put into a position like that, regardless of whether you've been clinically dead for two minutes or a split second. But I know that one minute I was in absolute pain and the next minute I experienced total peace, and if that was dying, and I believe it was, then dying is going to be really good.

It's fear about our transition from life to death that causes our transition to be difficult, believe me. The first time I was going, when I saw the grey crosses and felt caught in that negative, grey sand, I was scared out of my wits. But when I said to Mum, 'I'm going home,' I was okay with it. I was just instantly there in that beautiful white light and unconditional love.

When I woke up after that amazing experience I was strapped in bed, just to protect myself. I had a CAT scan that afternoon and that was very scary. I wasn't scared of dying, but I was thinking of my boy – who was going to look after him? So I had the CAT scan, all the trimmings, the whole caboodle, and they couldn't find anything wrong. My blood pressure was back to normal, temperature back to normal, and I felt quite relaxed. This was the drug doing its thing; it would have its waves, its highs and its lows.

Mentally and physically I was still very sore, but I understood that it was toxins from the chemicals after a year and a half on the drug, and it would hide in my system until it was ready to poke its head out and then it'd put me into a spin again.

I'm not denying that this is a drug that greatly helps some people, but for me it was totally the wrong thing; it just seemed to stuff up my system.

I tried to go the Human Rights Commission but they didn't want to know. I didn't have any luck going back to the doctors who'd prescribed the drug in the first place. They just denied that my problems could be related to this medication. I went back to see them when I got better, just to say 'Hey, you guys made a really bad call here' but then I realised I wasn't getting anywhere, so what was the point.

I just wanted them to see what they'd done. It took away nearly two years of my life, and then another year of recovery. In fact I still have convulsions from it, eight years later. If I get a fright, if I'm really tired, I could end up on the floor and just flip out.

I want people to know that all I have today, my spiritual abilities, didn't come out of the sky. I worked hard emotionally, physically and spiritually by being as positive as I can be. I've been at death's door three times. I've been left on the floor by ambulance drivers who thought I was a drug addict. I've been to hell and back (for want of words) to be where I am today because I trusted the light.

CHAPTER NINETEEN

'Why don't we share our gifts with those who need help?'

AFTER THAT terrible experience at Auckland Hospital I slowly began to heal, although it was a very hard road. About seven or eight months after it I began thinking that I really wanted to share with like-minded people about what had happened to me, about my spiritual journey. I also really wanted to get my confidence back.

Through a Tauranga friend I was put on to people involved with the Auckland spiritualist centres and began going along on Sunday evenings, just to listen at first. As I watched the other speakers, I began to develop my own ideas about the gift of seeing spirit, and the way in which I wanted to use it to help people.

What I saw was that people really needed to know that their loved ones were okay, but it seemed to me that no one could explain it very well. There were some good mediums, don't get me wrong, but I didn't always feel they had thought through the clearest, most respectful ways of passing on their messages. So, before I began standing up myself in these meetings, I had developed my own ideas about what worked and what didn't from a performance point of view.

I once watched a lady who did colour readings push her way into the audience and confront someone really directly, getting in their face with a message: 'You've got the colour yellow!' I thought a more respectful approach would be appropriate to the setting, such as: 'I'd like to come to you … this is what I think …' I also decided it was inappropriate for me to leave the stage while giving messages.

Or, in another instance, one medium gave a message to a woman: 'There's a frying pan hovering beside your head!' The client understandably said, 'What do you mean there's a frying pan there?' and the medium just said, 'Well I don't know, there's just a frying pan hovering there,' which isn't very helpful. Eddie and I were up the back laughing, with Eddie saying, 'Cook me some eggs!'

We had a really good time, not belittling anyone but we couldn't believe half of what these people were coming out with.

We're all gifted in our own way, but when you try to branch out into something that you're not talented in, it becomes very difficult and it's called ego. When your ego gets hold of you and you try to step up to the mark but you haven't actually worked your way there, you can't be expected to have all the answers.

So we watched mostly elderly people giving messages, many of whom were fantastic and highly respected in the Spiritualist Church of New Zealand. But some of them were very set in delivery style, and I felt the messages needed to be more refined. It was good, but it could be better.

From watching all these people I learnt many lessons and what not to do – never to expect anything to happen; never to allow my ego to take over; that spirit will give you what needs to be given and it's not up to you.

I began talking to groups of spiritual people at these churches. I'd talk about what my life had been like, and I did a few readings as well, which was fun. Word got out that I was able to connect pretty well and so I did the Auckland area circuit.

One week I'd go to Mangere Spiritual Church, the next it would be Ponsonby Spiritual Centre, then all over Auckland and Silverdale, even to Te Atatu, Manurewa, Howick. Most people don't realise there's a network of spiritual people, all over the country. They're really friendly places, and are all run on koha, with a cup of tea after-wards. Getting into this world was amazing as I'd grown up knowing nothing about it, but just having those experiences.

If you're a guest speaker, you do an address and you might want to do a reading from a book, and then they sing a song and then you do some readings. My confidence started to grow. I was asked to go to all these places, and all the while Eddie was down the back of the room, pulling faces at me.

Eddie is someone who is very on to it, and has the ability to do readings, but he just does his own thing. He likes to keep it close and would never get up on a platform. Without his friendship I wouldn't be able to focus as much as I can now. He'd be down the back doing silly stuff and making faces at me, but of course I wasn't allowed to laugh because everyone was looking at me. It taught me to focus on what I was doing. I loved it – I was doing full-on readings. It was great.

But I still wasn't 100 percent health-wise. I remember once in those early days I was doing some readings at a spiritual meeting in Manurewa. It was a small group, just in a school room, and I said to Eddie, 'I don't feel good.'

'Oh no, mate, you can't do that, not now,' he said.

'Nah, it's not good,' I said. I knew what was about to happen. 'We'll just go for a little walk.'

So we went for a walk around a couple of buildings and I had a mini seizure, shaking like a leaf, went into convulsions, managed to breathe through it, picked myself up, shook myself out a bit, said some prayers, went back in and nailed some readings, just like that. Afterwards, I got back into the car and had another convulsion.

It wasn't at all easy. People only saw me as this guy who could read people, but the thing is I was still pretty unwell. I just had a huge determination to be *me*. I had fought for my life and was still fighting to get back on track. I wanted to prove to myself that I was truly seeing these things. Inside, I was still fighting those people who had put me on medication to stop me seeing the spirit. They bloody near killed me, but they didn't stop me.

During readings people in the groups would say, 'Oh my god, that's my Dad, he cut his finger off ... and he had the scar on his back from the fallen tree, and how on earth do you know this stuff?'

'It's because he's standing here.'

I was so determined to prove myself correct, especially after so many people I loved had turned their backs on me because they didn't understand it, or believe me.

There was one experience where I learnt a really hard lesson. It happened at the Milford Spiritual Centre, which I particularly loved. The people who ran it at that time were really good to me and very understanding of what was going on in my life. So when they invited me to speak, I really wanted to do a good job.

I drove there with Eddie and a few friends, and we were talking and laughing all the way, and when we arrived and walked in I felt ten foot tall and bulletproof. I stood up the front and ... nothing.

'Oh,' I said, 'they're all standing back for some reason; they're not coming in to talk to me. I don't understand what's going on.'

'It's all right, dear,' this old lady at the very front said sympathetically, 'we all have days like that.'

Do you think I could read? Do you think I could get any messages out? Do you think I made myself look like an idiot? I was gutted, and mortified to think they wouldn't come to talk to me. I walked straight out and didn't talk to anybody. I was embarrassed and angry with

Right: Diving from Mt Maunganui beach with my mate. We're probably about fifteen years old.

Below: We went camping every year. Here we caught snapper and crays off the Coromandel Peninsula.

Left: A very cute Javan and me.

Below: I love this photo. Fishing in Te Kaha with my boy in 1995.

My Mum Heather and me.
Fishing in the Bay of Islands.

Heather and Javan,
Morrinsville, 1997.

Above: Maihimahi (Dolphin Fish), 18.2 kg, Tonga.

Left: Snapper, 24 pounds, Bay of Island. Fishin' is freedom.

Opposite top: I love this one. My mates and I went diving off the Coromandel. We found our secret hot spot.

Opposite bottom: Javan's first trout, Rotorua. He is four years old.

JC and me, 1998.

The view from the hotel I worked in, Vava'u, Tonga, 1997. A spiritual place.

Me and my big brother Murray, 1998.

Me and Colin after filming *6ixth Sense* in Kent, mid-summer 2004. I was buzzin'.

myself – exceptionally angry with myself.

I got home and threw my toys out of the cot. 'I'm never doing this again, I don't understand why they would do that to me, it made me look like a right womble ...' and on and on.

Eddie just said, 'It's part of your discipline.' And I just looked at him. It took me about six weeks of sitting working out what the issue was. When I did, I realised it was because I hadn't done my prayers before I went in. My ego had got away with me, and I'd gone in there *expecting* to talk to spirit, and wanting to prove myself. Spirit taught me the most valuable lesson that day, and that is discipline, because if you expect something spiritual to happen, it won't.

Now I never do a show without a prayer for permission to read in that place, for protection. In some of the venues we do now it takes half a day to do the prep. Some buildings you can walk into and I'll say, 'Kia ora guys, how you going, do you mind if I read? Not a problem? Choice, let's go!' And I'll put out a prayer and go on. But I never forget the time I didn't do it and was humiliated and extremely let down by my lack of discipline.

It wasn't long before I began to get frustrated by the limitations of the spiritualist churches. Spiritualist churches are like any other kind of church – if you speak there, you're preaching to the con-verted. Also, as in most groups, there were internal rivalries that I felt sometimes took precedence over what I thought we should be doing, which was using our gifts to help as many people as possible.

I began speaking out in the meetings, saying things like, 'There are a lot of people in this spiritual centre who I believe have a wonderful gift. Why don't you share these gifts with people on the outside who need the help? God's given you this blessing – why don't you share it? Bring someone along with you perhaps who's never been.'

Eventually, they didn't ask me back. That was a huge turning point for me, and pushed me into the life that I now lead where I have very little to do with other spiritually gifted people. That's not because

I don't think those people are amazing. I do think many of them are very gifted, but it wasn't a situation I easily fitted into. My own journey was taking me in a different direction.

What I wanted to do with my ability was to help people who didn't understand spirit, and to educate about life after death. Many people live in fear of death – their own and that of loved ones, and I want to help those people. I couldn't do that in a forum where people already had a set belief system, such as in a spiritualist church. They already knew that spirit existed, and that their loved ones were around them, so I felt that in that situation my gift was taking me around in circles.

So I prayed and I said 'What do you want me to do?' The word that came back to me again very clearly was 'media', and that was it.

'What do you mean, media?'

'Media, Kelvin, that's the way.'

'Do I go out actively looking for it?'

'No.'

And of course, eventually that's exactly what happened. The opportunities came to me unsought – all I needed was my faith.

As I started to feel healthier, I got myself a job working part-time as a chef in a restaurant not far from our house. I told them I'd been ill, and didn't want anything too hardcore – so I started on about 25 hours a week and worked up to 40. It helped get me back on my feet. Sometimes, though, I was still quite crook.

I remember times when I was running the restaurant (when the head chef had his days off) and I'd say, 'Hey boys, grab the pans' and fall on the floor, convulsing. Then they'd pick me up and ask, 'You all right, mate?' 'Yeah, good as gold', and I'd carry on.

I wasn't supposed to drive a car. I had my licence revoked for a year because of my tendency to flip out, and I had a few close calls.

At the same time, thanks to the spiritualist churches, word was getting around that I could read really clearly, and people were starting to ring me up and come to the house for readings.

CHAPTER TWENTY

Psychic chef

'CAN I be really honest with you?' I asked a customer one day. 'I actually do something else other than make coffees.'

It was a little further down the track and I was feeling much better, so I'd left the restaurant and got a job from 7 a.m. to 2.30 p.m. in the city, Monday to Friday, just running a wee café in a trendy part of town, in among lots of advertising and design companies, right next to the Saatchi and Saatchi offices.

People would come in and say, 'Morning', and I'd say, 'Morning', and then someone else would come in and greet me with 'Morning' and I'd reply in the same vein. I could see that although they worked right next door to each other they didn't know each other and they wouldn't even talk to each other.

Next day they came in, I'd say, 'Gidday, what's your name?'

'Oh, it's Mark.'

And the other fellow would come in. 'I'm Graham.'

I'd say, 'Hey Mark, have you met Graham? You work next to each other.'

'Oh I've seen you around blah blah' – and next thing you know, they're good mates. That's something that I really love doing, bringing people together. How could you go to the same coffee house, and work right next door to each other for 15 years, and not talk to each other?

At the same time I was making people's coffees I'd be seeing spirit – their dad, or their mum, or their nana. But I couldn't say anything because I was just a guy working in a café.

One customer was Ange. We became quite friendly, chatting away, so one day I decided to come clean.

'What else do you do?' she asked.

'Take it however you like but I tend to see things – people who have passed over and stuff, and there have been so many people trying to talk to you for ages, I can't hold my tongue anymore. Would you mind one day if we had coffee outside when I'm on a break and I'll have a talk to you?'

'Oh my god, that would be so cool!' she said.

So a day or so later we had a cup of coffee and all these people came through for her. As a result she told a few friends, and then all the other office girls would come down and ask, 'Do you have anything for me?' and I'd say, 'Oh well, blah blah blah'. So we sold a few extra coffees and things started to build up.

I suggested to my boss – a lovely Welsh woman called Carys – that we set up a barbecue at the café on Fridays in the summer, crack open a few mussels, what have you. People could line up and I'd give them a quick, two-minute reading as they walked through for the barbie.

It worked well and business took off for her, too, which was cool.

Then I came up with an idea that would combine both my skills: 'Psychic Chef'. This was where I went into people's houses, made some platters for them, a selection of whatever they wanted, or I'd cook for them or teach them cooking. And I'd do readings after they had their meal.

I'd charge for the food and for the reading. Bevan, one of the guys that I'd met in the café, had produced a flyer for me to help market Psychic Chef, because at that stage I didn't know how to use a computer. But what happened was people said they really just wanted me to do the readings. I was cool with that because I really wanted to get out of cooking.

In the end, one of the women who worked with me in the café said, 'Why do you even bother coming to work? It's just a waste of time. You should just be doing your spooky stuff.'

'Yeah,' I said, 'but I don't know if I can function without feeling normal.'

'You're not normal! Go and do your spooky stuff! People want you, go and do it.'

I was scared to go out on my own, but I gave it lots of thought and decided to just go for it – I'd wing it, trust the universe.

I rented a wee office on College Hill, close to the centre of the city, and began doing readings. People just turned up, and then sometimes people wouldn't turn up. So there were highs and lows, and I'd pray and pray because 'guys, I need to pay some bills'.

Myself and other psychics are sometimes criticised for taking money for reading. It can sometimes build expectations for the client: I'm paying money therefore I want to see some spirits. I don't run like that. Okay, I get paid to do a reading, but if the spirit doesn't come through they walk out with their cheque in their hand and it doesn't bother me because I'm not here to take people's money, I'm here to help. But I'm also here to support my family in a business. I've got bills to pay, too. I can't live off fresh air.

The money issue is quite a big thing for some people. But at the end of the day you don't get a builder to build a fence and not pay him. It's the same thing. I have a very good skill, why not charge?

Mostly, my clients would come at the right time and the bills would be paid. Then I started doing psychic parties. I'd travel to someone's house, and they'd organise a group of family or friends, anywhere between six and 10 people. I'd do readings for everyone who wanted, and charge them $50.

One lady came up to me after spirit and I had done an amazing reading and spoken with many of her family members who had all passed, and she stood there with tears in her eyes, opened her cheque book and said, 'That was priceless. How much do you need to get by?'

'Fifty dollars,' I said. 'That's it.'

'That's nothing,' she said. 'I'll leave the cheque open for you.'

'No way, my charge is fifty dollars, that's all.' People were so blown away by what was taking place in the readings that they would literally just open their cheque books, but I never took advantage of it. What was the point?

Some people in this world just want to know if they're going to get a new boyfriend or win Lotto or whatever. Sometimes at those psychic parties I would come across people with those expectations, but it's just not what I do. It doesn't work like that. I'm not a fortune teller; I see people who've passed over and that's just where it's at.

Grief is in everybody's own back yard and people have to deal with it in their own way. I can't tell anyone how to grieve and I certainly can't take away their pain. However, when spirits come through, it can be a tremendous part of the healing process, and very reassuring. Spirits can't live our lives for us, not at all, but they can certainly help us understand a little bit better.

One of the most powerful stories that came out of the psychic parties was that of a seven-year-old boy who had passed of a heart attack. His spirit came forward during one of those parties, and he was a very powerful little spirit. He told me the whole story himself. There were about half a dozen people at this party, all related.

The little boy came through and he started off with his cousins, then his uncle and then his aunty, and then his grandmother and he went round and he told them all these little secrets and they were all saying, 'Oh no, don't', and freaking out a bit, but it was lots of fun. Then he came to his mother last of all, and the story came out.

His mum had put him to bed one night but he came out and he said, 'Mum, I'm not feeling very well.'

'You'll be all right, just get back into bed, I'll come see you in a minute,' she said. She was watching the telly. As you do.

Twenty minutes later she was still watching her programme. She didn't go to him during the ads because she made a cup of tea instead. She'd thought, it's all quiet, he must be asleep. But he came out again.

'Mum, I'm just not feeling very well.'

'Well come here, sit on my lap,' because she wanted to watch her programme. I think any parent would understand this. Almost every time, this would be a perfectly respectable response.

So he hopped up and he cuddled into her. He was only seven, just wanted a cuddle, that's all he wanted. Then he kind of jumped. She looked down and she said, 'Are you all right?'

And he said, 'No, mum, I'm not,' and he died right there and then of a heart attack, in her arms.

You can imagine, everyone in the room was in tears. I was in tears trying to read for her and explain to her that it wasn't her fault. You could just see this immense pain leave her. There were black clouds over her – the guilt she carried of that dreadful experience had overpowered her and she basically wanted to take herself out. She couldn't deal with it. But then her son came through, and he proved to us who he was, and she was able to come to peace with it.

When people ask me why I do what I do it's simply because of experiences like that.

That was a beautiful time of my life, in 2004, when I was 33. I had gone through that really hard, black, dark time but was now feeling a lot better and had come off the medication. I was doing really well spiritually and financially I was okay, not too many worries.

At first, after I had committed myself to a spiritual life, I was over-whelmed by them. It was as if all the spirit people were just so excited that I was there and able to bring them forward, that they forgot I'm only human. For them, time doesn't exist, so they used to annoy me 24/7. In the end, I took control and told them that if they wanted me to work with them they had better get organised. Now we have formed a team, it runs more smoothly and I can live my life too.

I also learnt that it was best to try and understand what they were saying so that I could sleep at night. Then I wouldn't hear 'Kelvin wake up, Kelvin wake up' all the time. Now I was helping them, they no longer needed to get in my face. On the odd occasion if the mes-sage is urgent they'll tell me, though ... forewarned is forearmed.

Doing readings can be incredibly draining, but with the psychic parties I had plenty of down time. I'd have two days off in between them, maybe a few readings on those days, with lots of meditating and just being really relaxed.

Eddie moved back to Rotorua. I was still living in the house, but I couldn't afford to pay the rent by myself so I ended up moving in with Julie, an old friend from my cheffing days in Hamilton. Julie's house was out in Titirangi, a beautiful suburb set among the bush to the west of the city.

One day I was sitting in my office in College Hill when a young woman came in for a reading. She seemed really nervous, so I was putting her at her ease, saying, 'How are you going, come on in', and setting up the tape recorder. I always tape the readings so that clients can take the tape away with them later.

Suddenly I said to her, 'You've got a camera in your bag.'

'No I haven't.'

'Yes you have.' And we to'd and fro'd like that for a bit. She kept saying, 'I don't know what you're talking about.'

But if I closed my eyes and focused with my third eye, all I could see were wires and the switchboard of a TV panel – like a control panel at a TV station.

'I'm pretty sure you've got a camera in your bag and I'm pretty sure you've got a microphone in your shirt somewhere,' I said. 'Can you move your bag?'

'You must be nuts,' she said, and refused to move her bag from where she'd placed it.

'Okay then,' I said, 'I think it might be *Target*.' *Target* is a television show that tries to entrap people by filming them when they don't know they're being filmed. I leaned forward, with my face close to the bag, and waved. 'Hi, Mum!' Then I sat back, and we continued with her reading.

Sure enough, two weeks later I received a letter from *Target* stating, 'We caught you on camera' and implying that nothing I'd said had made any sense to the 'client'. The way they constructed the letter made me look really bad. I was devastated at their deceit; it made me feel really, really bad, completely useless. Realistically, I should've thrown her out right from the start, but oh no, as usual I felt I had to prove to everybody that I could see dead people.

I'm not a person who's out to deceive anybody. All I could think was, how could you do that to me, deliberately set out to make me look bad? So I left the office feeling broken, thinking that was the end of my career.

It felt like a real kick in the guts, especially after all I'd been through with the drugs. When was I going to get a break? What did I have to do in this world to make things right for my son and for me and for people around me?

I moved out of my central office and just hung around in Titirangi, becoming a bit of a hermit. People came out to the house and I did readings from the house. I wasn't on the dole or anything, I was supporting myself, but I disappeared off the radar.

Six months later, the *Target* programme went to air and I was incredibly nervous about what they were going to say about me. They said, 'We've got three clairvoyants and this one did this and this one did this but *this* one we're not too sure if it's his keen eye of observation, or whether he does have a spiritual gift, because this is what he said: 'It must be *Target* in there. Hi Mum!' And they played it – they played the critical point of 'you must have a camera in your bag'. That's all they played. I was the first person in the country ever to catch their cameras. You can't actually see the cameras, so they didn't know how I'd done it. My career went through the roof. I sat there crying with relief after six months of stressing out.

I've since met people who knew that girl from *Target*, and while the things that I said to her didn't make sense at the time, they did ultimately come true. A lot that spirit told her in the reading happened. That's psychic awareness. You don't always understand what's being said, but it usually comes out in the wash sooner or later.

I used to wrestle a lot with self-doubt. Not now. I now know that I'm blessed every day, and I've learnt so much more about the way spirit works. We don't always understand what spirit is saying to us, and it can be quite frustrating in a show where the messages are coming but nobody understands what I'm saying.

People might respond, 'We don't know what you're talking about,' but the following week someone might say something to them and they'll realise what I was talking about. We get a lot of emails like this.

So things took off again, and I carried on doing the psychic parties. It was full on, and I loved every minute of it. I just used the money I made from one party to get me to wherever the next one was. I was driving all over the place, sometimes hundreds of kilometres, in my old bomb, a Nissan hatchbacky thing I'd named Isabella. She had a blue door that leaked like a sieve, and if it rained we got wet. That thing used to fly!

One day I was driving to a psychic party, a family group down in Hamilton, and I was thinking about things, and recognising that I was getting to a point where I needed some change. I put it out there, spiritually. I said, 'I'm really frustrated, I don't know what I should be doing, I need somebody to help me out.' And I swear I heard this voice say, 'You must go to England.'

CHAPTER TWENTY-ONE

'Everyone needs a break in their life.'

'YOU MUST go to England.'

The voice was crystal clear, as if someone was sitting in the back of the car. I thought to myself, 'What? I don't want to go to England!' It hadn't been on my mind at all, and I didn't feel any desire to go.

By this stage I had a mobile phone – it was like a brick – and at that moment it rang. It was an English friend of mine, a spiritual lady who does Reiki.

'Hello love, how are you doing? I've just been doing some meditation and they're telling me you're going to England.'

'Get away, I've literally just had that message from above.'

'Well,' she said, 'it doesn't surprise me because they're adamant you're going to England.'

Okay, I thought, that's a bit weird. I went down to Hamilton, did the psychic party, stayed the night at my Dad's and was driving back the next day when another friend rang up and said, 'I had this wicked dream about you last night. They told me to tell you that you've got to go to England.'

'No way!' That was the three, the big three, and I thought to myself, 'How do I get there, what do I do?'

That was on the Sunday. Monday morning, my landline phone rang.

'Hi, Kelvin, it's so-and-so here from the *Western Leader* newspaper. We've been hearing some good things about your work and we want to do an editorial on you.'

'I can't afford that,' I said, naïve as anything.

'No, no, it's on us!'

He came over that very day, did an interview, took some photos and asked, 'What do you want to do with your gift?'

'I just want to help people,' I said. Since those phone calls over the weekend, I'd been thinking about England, and the possibility of actually going there, and to Europe. So I told this reporter, 'Colin Fry, the world's most famous psychic medium, has a college in Sweden called the International College of Spiritual Science and Healing. I would really, really like to go and learn from him.' That had become my goal.

Colin Fry had been on afternoon television here, and I used to watch his television show *6ixth Sense*. There was always a great debate about how this guy could do what he did, and he just inspired me to keep going. He inspired me to be true to myself. I also thought, if he could be up there on a set doing it, why couldn't I? What's stopping me from being the first Kiwi to have his own medium show? It was very inspirational for me.

A couple of days later there was a big spread in the editorial section of the newspaper, and the story said I was a psychic medium who specialised in helping people communicate with their loved ones who had passed on. It was a very sympathetic article, and mentioned that I wanted to go to Colin Fry's college. Well, the phone rang off the hook and I did 428 readings in 12 weeks. I saved enough money to pay all my bills, fly to Colin's college in Sweden and then fly to England to see some friends – and get home. But just two weeks before I was due to fly to Sweden, Colin's college emailed and said that due to the scheduling of his TV programme, Colin wouldn't be there to teach at the time I was booked in, but that there were all these other wonderful mediums who would be there.

I could scarcely believe what was happening. I was crying into the computer, and emailed back to say that I didn't think there was any point in my coming to Sweden if Colin wasn't going to be there. I was bawling my eyes out.

Colin himself emailed me back and said, 'I'm so sorry but there are other good mediums and I'm really apologetic …'

And I replied, saying, 'Thank you very much but I'm going to decline because it's a long way for me to come and I was hoping to learn from you because I believe that you're truly gifted. I'm still going to go to England because I've paid for my tickets and that was a lot of money for me, but I'm just going to miss out on the Sweden thing.'

He emailed back, 'How about I shout you to my show and you just rock on up any time you like and we'll go from there. Here's my personal number.'

I flew to England with my backpack, and after two days I rang him.

'I'm just in the cab going to the show,' he said. 'I've got your name at the door and there's a five-day opportunity for you to turn up, and we'll make room for you.'

I took the train from London to Kent, through the beautiful English landscape that struck me as so elegant and pristine. I arrived at the theatre to find a queue of people outside. I walked straight into the main foyer, full of confidence, and said, 'I'm a guest of Colin's, my name's at the door.'

The girl on the door said, 'You have to go to the back of the line.'

'Oh, okay, cool as.' I cruised down the back of the line and eventually filed in, and had to sign release forms.

The studio was packed with people, all full of anticipation. Meanwhile, I had dead people coming at me from all directions.

I got into the theatre where his show was being filmed for a global audience, and I started to cry. I was just so overwhelmed that for the first time in my life I'd had a dream and I was living it. Oh my goodness, I was in England, on the set of Colin Fry, it felt primo. I was just really happy and the tears were falling down my face, and this old lady next to me put her hand on mine and said, 'It's all right dear, I'm sure if they come through Colin will find them for you and I'm sure they're absolutely fine and they love you. It'll be all right.'

'Oh. Thanks!' But of course I wasn't crying because of that. I was just overwhelmed. There I was, sitting in the theatre with 250 people waiting to see the man who was a legend to me.

Colin came out and started reading. He began by talking about a gentleman who'd passed who was really well known for making little model cars out of wood – and my heart just dropped. He said, 'I'm trying to find the owner of this one, he's come a long way.' He didn't know I was in the audience, he certainly didn't know I was coming on that day.

'Now,' he said, 'there's a little boy he's trying to give the little toys to, and the little boy's blonde, blue eyed and he's only about six.'

I was thinking, 'That's Great Pop, he's talking about Great Pop and Javan.' Great Pop was renowned for his model cars. He'd recently passed, about four months earlier.

As this was dawning on me, Colin, who had been side on to me, just turned and pointed to me and said, 'It's you, young man.'

'Could be,' I said. I was really blown away.

'He's for you. I think I need to invite you down on to the stage because this man really needs to talk to you. It's really important about your son.' At that stage, I was indeed having a lot of trouble around my son, and not being allowed to see him.

The cameras were rolling and I said, 'okay', and everyone was trying to get out of my way and I said, 'I've got to stick my shoes on first.'

Being a typical Kiwi, I'd taken my shoes off in the hot English summer. I put my shoes on and went down to the stage. As I did so Colin said, 'Are you Kelvin from New Zealand?', and I said, 'Yeah mate, kia ora!'

'Ladies and gentlemen, this is a young man who's travelled all the way from New Zealand to be here. I've given him tickets, but I didn't know who he was. From what I hear of him, he's a very good medium. Come on down.'

So I came down to the stage and sat on the couch. Goodness, invited to sit down on the couch next to Colin! This was just too much. He was talking but I have no idea what he said. All I could think was, oh my god, I'm sitting next to Colin Fry. He read, and he said something about 'this gentleman's talking about cooking eggs … I've got eggs for Africa', and I said, 'I'm an ex-chef, mate.' He talked about Javan, that he was going to be safe and get through some of the stuff he was going through.

The reading finished and I went back into my seat and the old lady next to me said, 'See, told ya.' Cheeky old Doris.

Afterwards, I had to go to the green room where they interviewed everyone who'd had a reading with Colin and asked us what the experience meant to us. I was waiting with all the other people for my turn to go in. I presumed we were all like-minded, so when a lady said to me, 'So you're a medium from New Zealand?' I said, 'Yeah, do you want me to tell you about it?' Colin had read for her and picked up on her Dad but he'd missed the mother and the sister and the aunty and Joan and Frank – so away I went.

I was still talking to these people when Colin and another woman came into the room and walked over to me. 'Hi,' she said, 'I'm from ITV. We've actually been watching you because we have cameras in here, and Colin and I have decided that we'd really love you to be a guest on the show.'

'*What?*' My face dropped. 'When?' And she said, 'Twenty minutes.'

'I don't think I can do it,' I said. 'I think I'm just too emotional. I can't believe it' – and I burst into tears. I'd worked so hard to be accepted, and had gone through all the drugs stuff and been through so much – and here was Colin, who was such a hero to me, asking me to be a guest.

'Can I do it tomorrow?' I asked. The next day they sent a chauffeured Jaguar to pick me up. I'd never been in a Jaguar before. This time there was no standing in the queue. I was a special guest and I walked straight through.

As I was standing out the back with Colin Fry, I was overwhelmed by the whole experience.

'You'll be right, mate, just do your thing,' he told me. Then he went out on stage in front of the cameras and said, 'Ladies and gentlemen, please welcome our special guest all the way from New Zealand, Kelvin Cruickshank' – and I walked out.

I began, 'Hi, hi everybody, I'm Kelvin from New Zealand. Obviously I work a little differently from Colin but we'll give it a crack. Gidday, sir, how are you going? Okay, I've got this young bloke coming through, he tells me his name's Michael, does that mean anything to you because I need to acknowledge the Michael with you, sir ...'

The man said, 'That's my name. You're talking to my son.'

'Oh right,' and away I went.

I did four other reads, five altogether, but they were little short ones because I'd felt like I'd done what I needed to do. Colin came out and everyone clapped. It was overwhelming.

Afterwards, he said, 'You did really well. For a young fellow, that's pretty amazing stuff. We're glad we've given you the opportunity, and everyone needs a break in their life.'

He didn't say much more to me but those words 'everybody needs a break' meant so much to me.

I then left, but spent two days crying because I couldn't remember what I'd done. I been so up in the clouds and was left with an awful feeling I'd done something really bad, that I'd failed – how stupid.

I left England and went to Italy with an Italian/Australian friend Elena who speaks Italian. Wherever we went, Elena would tell these Italian people, 'This is my friend Kelvin, he sees dead people.' She'd translate, and we'd end up captivating entire restaurants, or train carriages. We'd meet people and they'd ask what I did, and I'd say, 'I've just been on Colin Fry's show.' I had beautiful experiences in Italy. I read all over the country.

An especially powerful thing happened as Elena, I and two other girls were leaving La Cinque Terre to head back to Rome. La Cinque Terre is part of the rugged stretch of coast on the Riviera, and we'd been there a little bit too long, because it was just so beautiful. I was sleeping out underneath the olive trees and I had the presence of angels. It's the closest to feeling completely safe that I've ever felt.

We were waiting for the train, sitting in this country station, and having a pizza. Elena said, 'Are you alright? You look a bit faint.'

'Yeah, I'll just sit here with my eyes closed for a minute,' I said. And *boof*! – I was literally thrown right into the middle of a dream or a vision. In this vision I was with the same friends and we had reached a different train station, one with large arches. We had to get out of that station, walk through the arches, walk through an open courtyard, then through a tunnel to get to the next station, and then we had to wait. Now, of course, Italy has statues of the Virgin Mary everywhere, but, at the very end of the platform there was this Mother Teresa statue. Everything was cool. But then I started to get all panicky.

There was a boy sitting on a bench across from these railway tracks, in a pair of jeans, a hat and a white shirt, with a backpack, writing in one of his books. He was reading a book and then writing a bit, reading and then writing a bit.

Then a woman walked out of the public toilets nearby. She had big, frizzy hair and a bag whose strap fell diagonally across her body, and she was wearing a crucifix on her necklace. She was a very dark girl, from a different culture.

Then all of a sudden this skinhead guy approached her. He had army pants on, and he was trying to get a cigarette off her. He looked like he was loaded, off his nut, and I started to get really nervous about it.

In my vision, the four of us friends were all just sort of standing around, and the message came to me: leave your backpacks on; if he gets on the train, get off. End of the story.

At that point I came to and explained the whole thing in detail. I said to the girls, 'I don't understand this. It may happen today, it may happen next year, but what I do know, if that guy gets on the train we get off.'

We arrived in Rome and had to change trains. We went through some arches and by now the girls were thinking, 'Mate, didn't you just tell us about this back there?'

'Yeah, just keep our wits about us.' We went through this tunnel and out, and there was Mother Teresa at the very end of the centre aisle with two train lines and there were people sitting around and there was a boy with a white shirt and a hat, reading and writing in his book. The girls said, 'Oh my god, look there's that boy. What's going on?' And they all started getting really nervous.

'Look, it will be okay,' I said, 'we'll just stay close together.' By now it was quite late at night, with hardly anyone round. Out of the public toilets came the girl with the frizzy hair, and the olive skin and the satchel. It was so precise it wasn't funny. The guy in army pants, the camo stuff, skinhead, loaded, walked out from around the corner of the building that we'd come through, and bailed up this woman really badly. It was as if he was out to kill, he was so aggressive. Everyone there just froze. The girls started to cry, but I was trying to remind them that we'd been shown we'd be fine. If he got on the train, we got off.

The train eventually came in and we jumped on. 'Leave your backpacks on, guys,' I said, 'don't sit down, let's just stand up, just in case.' So, we stood there at the far end of the carriage by the other door. The doors closed and we breathed a sigh of relief. But just in that same instant, an arm came through, pulled the door and the skinhead jumped on the carriage with us, and the train moved off.

He threw himself down into a seat next to the same girl that he'd spoken to on the platform. There was another guy sitting across from her. Everyone on the carriage was trying not to look at him.

We got off at the very first stop and the train carried on. It was so late there were no more trains and we had to walk, but it was worth it to be away from that situation.

There were two main things I took away from that vision – firstly that I had shared it. I didn't understand it but I spoke about it. I suppose I was learning the lesson from all those years before, when as a small child I'd had the visions of Joe burning, and not told anyone about it. Secondly, to have the experience actually physically take place I learned that I had to trust my visions and not deny them.

It was an incredible warning. If we hadn't been prepared, we could have got ourselves into trouble. Who knows what would have happened if I had ignored the vision.

Although I loved Italy, there were things about it I found quite difficult – lots of earth-bound negative stuff. I found being in trains, going through tunnels very uncomfortable, full of souls that I wouldn't allow into my psyche because they would just override me. I knew they were there so I just clamped on my Discman – no iPods in those days, couldn't afford one – and played my CDs, the louder the better.

I listened to a lot of *Nickleback* in those tunnels – a real hard rock band but with quite positive lyrics.

Then there was Rome itself. I went to the Coliseum and cried the whole way around. I wanted to get out, but instead of running away from it I did a massive prayer, and told the spirit that if there were any of them lost and they wanted to go through, they could. That was an experience and a half. I felt very humble.

It was very hot when we were in Rome, and there were lots of wee bottle stores so I had a few beers. Typical Kiwi. Then I saw a swimming pool. Choice! Everyone was sort of wetting their hands and dangling their feet, but not me. I went straight in. It was only shallow but I was hot. There was money all over the bottom of the pool, but I didn't take any of it – I just wanted a dip.

What I didn't realise was it was the Trevi Fountain, and there were security guards everywhere. My first and last tongue-lashing from Italian police.

CHAPTER TWENTY-TWO

'Sensing Murder' calls

WHAT DO you do after you've been on the number one psychic show in the world? I returned to New Zealand and life just went on as usual. I didn't have any money but that's never bothered me. I needed somewhere to live, so I did a meditation and asked spirit and they said, 'Go for a drive to Cornwallis.'

Cornwallis is an extremely beautiful, tiny settlement on the shores of the Manukau Harbour. It's out in the west of Auckland – bush to the back, sea at the front. I went for a drive and saw the 'for rent' sign on a bach just across the road from the beach. There were big gaps around the windows, and the toilet was just a long drop outside, so it was pretty rough, but I didn't care. I moved in straight away and just hung out.

That kind of environment is perfect for me. I'd meditate on the verandah in the morning and the sun would come up and I loved it, it was great. I was swimming every day, getting scallops and fishing for food. I did a few readings. People used to drive all the way out there just to see me – it's a good 40 minutes from the city. They'd bring out groceries which was really helpful because I'd come back to nothing. The readings picked up, and I started doing some psychic parties again and things went from strength to strength.

I could work as many or as few hours as I wanted to. If I wanted a week off, then I'd take one. When Javan wasn't around I'd work quite hard and when he was around I didn't work at all. That's still what's happening with me now: I work extremely hard one week but the following one I'll work shorter hours to be home with my boy. I feel like I missed out on a lot with him, so I'm very conscious of spending quality time with him.

Not very long after I got back, in August 2004, I put on the TV (Mum had bought one for me and Javan) and found that Colin Fry's show was back on air. I watched his first set and then it went to ads. Then he came back on and first up, there I was. 'Ladies and gentlemen, please welcome Mr Kelvin Cruickshank!' The programme was screened around the globe – 16.8 million viewers saw that episode. It was insane.

I had been really worried about this moment. I really couldn't remember anything about how I'd done. But watching it now, I felt nothing but relief, total relief. They didn't play the shorter readings, which is fair enough. I was very young and I'd never ever been in front of a camera before and was quite overwhelmed by the situation. But the people that I read for first – their son had passed of leukaemia and he was about my age at the time – gave a great interview afterwards that just blew me away because I'd never really had the feedback before. They said, 'Kelvin's changed our lives, it's just so nice that our son's still here, he knows about us, we'll forever have Kelvin in our prayers.' That's pretty massive, when somebody says that to you.

Everything just went through the roof after that – lots of phone calls, lots of people wanting readings.

Dad rang about two weeks later. He never used to ring at all, although he does now.

'Boy, I saw you on the telly. Pretty bloody clever, aren't ya?'

'I don't know, am I?'

'Pretty amazing stuff.'

That was the turning point for my Dad. He'd always been a bit afraid of what he called 'this clairvoyant rubbish, dead people, rah, rah, rah' and very wary of his own abilities, yet preferring to have nothing to do with it. Now, here was his son on the best psychic show in the world and he was sitting there watching me for the first time in my work mode, gobsmacked.

He told me how he'd come to be watching it. 'I was out in my den getting ready to watch a horse race and the blooming remote wouldn't change to the right channel. It was stuck on TV ONE, and I was smashing up the remote and yelling at the girlfriend, and then it said, 'Ladies and gentlemen, please welcome Mr Kelvin Cruickshank' and I just said, "Look, Kelvin's on the TV".'

We started chatting a bit and I said, 'Actually Dad I'm doing some charity events, would you like some tickets?'

'Oh yeah, sure, tickets, sure.' He'd never been to visit me in Auckland, so I sent him some tickets and he and his girlfriend Barbara came up, which was a big deal for me.

I did three charity events over three nights at the end of 2004 – one each for the Blind Foundation, Starship Children's Hospital, and the Rescue Helicopter. Dad walked in to where I was doing the show and I just burst into tears. I was so stoked that he'd accepted me for the first time in my life.

I had a strong feeling that I wanted to give back, and I still do. I'm a sponsor of the Franklin Zoo, and cystic fibrosis.

I am extremely happy to be able to give money to organisations I believe in – happy and proud. For a kid who was told he would be nothing, and who was labelled 'dumb', that's pretty cool.

Lots of benefits came from appearing on Colin Fry's programme – I don't mean financially, but more in terms of sewing my heart back together. One benefit was to take my life in a completely new direction.

I received a phone call from a woman who told me her name was Yvonne Grace, and she was an associate producer with Ninox Television. She said a good friend of mine, Janice Priest from *Rainbow News*, New Zealand's mind, body and spirit magazine, had been in contact with them about me. 'She tells us you're a medium. We're putting together a show based on crime scenes,' Yvonne told me.

She carried on, describing the format of *Sensing Murder* that is now so familiar to us: where psychics with no prior knowledge of a cold case involving possible murder attempt to communicate with the spirits of the victims to find out what happened.

It was intriguing, but by this stage I was really quite determined not to be walked on anymore. Being on Colin Fry's show was the pinnacle for me, and it gave me the confidence to be very upfront about what I did and didn't want to do. Also, with television, you don't always know what tack they're going to take, and there was a chance that a show like she was proposing would be very exploitative and have a negative impact. So I listened to her and at the end I said, 'If it's positive, I might consider it,' and I agreed to go along to a meeting about it.

Just as I was about to get off the phone – and I was shaking like anything – I asked, 'What's the pay like?'

She said, 'What?'

'How much are you going to pay me to put my life at risk here?'

'We're not paying you,' she said. 'You'll get lots of exposure but we won't be paying you.'

And I said, 'Well, to be totally fair, then I'm not doing it.' I was trying to be businesslike but it was very hard to say that, especially when you've been brought up to believe if you've got a gift you should just give it. But I was just trying to stand up for myself.

'We'll have to consider that once we've had the meeting,' she said.

'Okay then, so long as you're prepared to consider it, because I'm not going to do it for nothing.'

I was still really good friends with Ange, the girl I'd done the first reading for back at the café in town. She's a very intelligent girl, so I rang her to see what she thought about it. We met up for coffee and a yak.

She said, 'Well, if it's positive and it helps people, like you always say to me, then why not?' was her answer. 'What are they paying you?'

'Initially they said they wouldn't pay anything.'

'No, no, no,' she said. 'You must put a figure in your head and you mustn't do it unless you get that figure.'

I told her the figure I had in my head, and she said, 'If that's what you want then that's how it will be and you don't do it for anything less.'

So I went to the interview in a hotel with Yvonne. She told me I was the last person they were interviewing, then she offered me a photo and asked me to tell her about it. I declined to look at the photo because in such situations I believe the person in spirit who has asked for help should be strong enough to manifest themselves to me. This way I can begin to trust that spirit person and form a relationship.

I don't do it to show off – but I do think that it proves again and again that if I haven't seen the photo then I *must* be seeing dead people. I find it an amazing challenge to describe and prove what the spirit person looked like in the living. It's a big puzzle and I like to work hard to work it out.

I began to talk. 'There's this person standing in the room …' and all this stuff came pouring out, and I revealed a case that was known to them but not to me, of course. She was sitting there, her eyes popping out of her head and she turned the photo over and there was the young girl in spirit I had just described, bang on. She was quite overwhelmed.

'Did that make sense to you?' I asked, and she said, 'Yes, we'll be in touch.'

'Oh, just before you go,' I said, 'If I do get the job, what are you paying me?'

'We've had discussions about that,' she replied, and she named a figure.

'That's fine, thank you,' I said, very coolly. It was the exact amount that I'd said to Ange.

Soon after, there was a phone call. 'We want to go forward with this, and we want to fly you to Wellington.'

I then met the big boss, and had another interview – more yakking away in the boardroom, and I was explaining to everyone what I did. At one point, I went to the bathroom and there in the corner was a young Maori girl who told me all this stuff about herself. 'This is my Maori name and this is what happened to me and they want you to work on my case but I'm too afraid of you because you're a boy because a boy killed me.' I was quite overwhelmed. Flippin' heck! So I went back to the boardroom and I said, 'I don't mean to be crossing the line here and I don't even know what your plans are, but there's this young Maori girl in the bathroom and she just told me all this stuff and she'd prefer for me not to work on her case.'

It was Olive Walker, whose case was to be the first to be high-lighted by *Sensing Murder* in New Zealand. Olive Walker was a shy, gentle, 18-year-old who was killed in Rotorua in 1970. No one was ever convicted for her murder. With me ruled out of the investigation by Olive herself, Australian psychic Deb Webber and New Zealand psychic Adelle Dishcombe were chosen, and both found that Olive had been abused and then killed by a male. The information she told me in that bathroom was bang on, and it made the people in the

172

boardroom pretty freaked out. They realised then that I could do this stuff. So I got the job.

They'd interviewed 75 people in New Zealand, and of those only three were selected, myself, Sue Nicholson and Adelle Dishcombe.

CHAPTER TWENTY-THREE

'I relive the experience'

I WAS so nervous I didn't sleep the night before.

My first case on *Sensing Murder* was George Engelbrecht, a lovely, lonely old man who had been beaten to death in his own home in Alicetown, a suburb near the northern reaches of Wellington harbour, back in 1979. All I was told was that it was a case of unsolved murder, nothing else, and I was flown to Wellington on the morning of the day that filming was due to start.

I asked the angels and the white light for protection and for the strength and the positive vibe to help me work though the murder cases. I pray for hours preparing for all the cases, as they are not very easy to do.

When George came through for me, he was able to tell me that there had been two people involved in his murder, rather than the lone man that police had thought. Another man had waited outside the house, keeping watch, and George told me that this second man had felt so guilty about the crime that he had since committed suicide.

This was completely new information, and investigations afterwards found that a local man who had been questioned about George's murder, and who'd been part of a group of youths who'd broken into George's home a year earlier, had actually hanged himself while in police custody for something else. That man's sister also came to visit me after *Sensing Murder* aired on television, and she told me that she had suspected her brother had been at George's house on the night of the murder.

Police have since said they couldn't rule out the possibility of there having been a second person involved. They said they had photographed an unusual boot print inside the house. They had never made that public, yet both Deb and I identified that there was something very unusual about the boot print.

Police investigations are continuing on the basis of the information we got from George.

He was a lovely man but he died a horrific death.

In those early episodes we were told that it was an unsolved murder but as the series progressed we weren't told even that. If, for instance, the body had never been located, and it had never been established that the person was actually dead – for instance, with Amber-Lee Cruickshank and Alexa Cullen – we were not told that, either.

The rules for the programme are pretty tight. We have no idea where we're going until we get to the airport that morning, and even then we might fly, say, to Queenstown, like we did for Amber-Lee Cruickshank, and then end up driving almost 50 kilometres to get to the murder scene. And that's all down to us. No one tells us where to go. We look at the map, pick up the area, and then we direct the driver of the car.

We work just one full day on every case – and that's it. It's sometimes really frustrating, because often you want to go deeper, do more – but you can't. The thinking behind that is that if it spread over more than one day, we might go away and research the case from other sources. As if! I swore to myself that I would never research anything and to this day I never have and I never intend to. I believe that if I'm blessed to be able to help someone then the spirit will give me the information and I trust that they will only ever give me what I'm supposed to be giving. You've got to trust the spirit because if you force it then it will never work.

Another reason for keeping it to a limited time frame is because it's so draining on us. We're basically doing the reading for nine hours or more, going through all sorts of violence and emotions, so it can be very exhausting. Sometimes I'll cry for a couple of weeks after doing one of these cases, because I can't get the images out of my head of what was done to the victim.

We're constantly supervised during that day and everything we do or say is recorded through microphones that we have to wear – we couldn't get away with anything, and none of us would ever want to or need to.

From the start, my motivation was extremely high to help the families of these victims. As a child I'd seen at first hand the destruction to families and communities that murder causes. The effects of the murder of Aunty Nola in Rotongaro back in the 1970s are still felt today. Uncle Don lost his life partner – he's never stopped missing her, and we all still talk about it. And that's not counting the effect on the murderer's family.

With my gift coming out stronger and stronger through my life, and with me being able to see all this stuff, I have to ask, how can I help?

That's why, when *Sensing Murder* first contacted me, my initial reaction was, 'If it helps people then I'm in. As soon as you start doing cheesy stuff I'm gone.' And so far it's been pretty good across the board.

Sensing Murder has helped in many ways. It re-opens many un-solved cases, most of which have been shelved, and many of them have not been covered by the media and never properly looked at. In some of the cases, I believe the cops have just shelved them.

If the police don't have the funds they don't really look into certain crimes. If they keep hitting dead ends then they just put their officers or their detectives into other areas and don't finish what they started, and that's because of the demands of their job, I suppose. The Alexa Cullen case is a good example of that. *Sensing Murder* took up the case, to bring it to the fore.

Sensing Murder helps the victims' families by providing answers and, through that, some sense of closure. And it helps the spirits to a sense of peace, and to pass on to the other side, once they have communicated what they know.

The families themselves approach *Sensing Murder* for help and in almost all cases the police have also asked us to help them. From my heart, I can't thank the families enough for being so strong and determined to get their stories out. They, the families, have to relive their emotions and feelings, all their hurt, anger and pain, and that can't be easy at all. They are the brave. My prayers are always with them.

As for the police, they have slowly allowed us to investigate. I have met some amazing people in the force and I would like to thank them for their sheer guts in standing up and being counted for what they as individuals believe. Some of those coppers have put their necks on the line for the families and the victims.

For me, as a medium, *Sensing Murder* is exceptionally draining. I get pretty tired doing four or five readings in the office a day, but I reckon one *Sensing Murder* case on one day is similar to two months' work. I'm absolutely stuffed afterwards.

First of all we start off with a photo of a victim and we connect with that person and find out a bit about them, get a sense of their personality. That's okay, but then we ask them to show us what happened to them and the energy shifts to the point of their fear and they relive it, so we become part of that. I can be in a hotel room somewhere doing the reading, but at that point I forget where I am because I'm so fixed on their journey. My vibrational tone becomes really high – hyper-sensitive if you like – and I relive the experience.

I've seen two and a half year old Amber-Lee Cruickshank have her neck broken because she wouldn't stop crying for her mother. To watch that in my mind is horrific. I've seen Kevin O'Loughlin stabbed many times over, and that's played out in my head. It may not be my reality as such, I'm not actually going through it, but I'm so close to observing what's taking place, it's extremely painful. I totally feel that pain and fear myself – I feel what's taking place because I've got to know what happened. That's why we're doing *Sensing Murder*.

For this to happen, I go into the dream state which I call 'the zone' – the feeling of being between wakefulness and sleep, only it's controlled. It's different from sleep-dreaming – you have the same sort of sensations as a dream but it's reality; it's somebody's child you're watching being strangled or whatever.

Seeing images from spirit, for me, is like having a TV inside my head that I can see with what I call my third eye. The images flicker, as if on fast-forward. With experience, I've learned more about how to watch what spirit sends me, because it's not like the normal way of seeing. It's not as straightforward, and it's all about feeling, as well.

I've seen people come into my space who have been shot and I'll stand here and I'll ask, 'Are you all right?' They're in the spirit world and they'll say, 'Look at my chest' and they'll reveal their chest and there's a gaping hole. More to the point they've got blood on their hands and they turn around and you can see the exit wound on the other side. The worst ones are the stabbings because they're really messy.

The hardest part of *Sensing Murder* is when we have to retrace the footsteps of the victim, and put it all into a sequence that includes the killer. Imagine the energy of someone who's got a secret that bad.

He's just dark – very, very dark. To get close to that person spiritually you must penetrate the darkness that surrounds them. The universal law states you are forbidden to take another's life. We are not here to do that, but it happens, and darkness surrounds those people, the criminals.

This is where my learning comes into play – the experiences I've had where I've learnt to recognise those negative energies. This is why I had to learn the hard way, so that I understand it now, that change of energy. I understand different concepts of lifestyle, different life experiences, and different spiritual energy forms – the dark side of things, demonic energies. That doesn't mean to say that I have them in my life now, because I don't, but I can recognise when we're in the dark zone and we've got to penetrate through it to find some of the answers regarding the person who may have been involved. Tattoos, the colour of their hair, what they look like, what they do, how old they are, are there any scars standing out? It's like standing in a fire: I can't sustain it very long and I've got to get out.

You have to be very careful dealing with these kinds of energies, and that's where discipline comes into play. The danger is great, and it can drain the life out of you. That's why some clairvoyants crash. That's why some people who have the skills fall over because they're not aware of how much the bad stuff has taken away their good stuff. It's a seesaw effect.

People often ask why spirit doesn't just come right out and say, such-and-such did it and here is their name and address. There are a couple of answers to that. One is that spirit often does give us names – those are the bits that get bleeped out by the programme's makers, because there's such a thing as due process, and you can't just go broadcasting someone's name on TV, saying they committed a murder. We pass all that information on to the police – and I think it's fair to say that the cops wouldn't ever like to say that a crime was solved because of evidence provided by the psychics.

With Alexa Cullen, Sue and I both came up with detailed descriptions of the murderer, his physical appearance and the job he did. Local residents recognised who it was. Police records also showed that a man who matched our descriptions had been jailed in 2000 for ill-treating a child. Alexa's spirit also provided the actual name of someone who she said knew the killer, and this was confirmed by relatives.

Sometimes, we get very clear messages about the killer's identity, but are stopped going any further. We did one case with a guy, Kevin O'Loughlin, who'd been stabbed many times and left to die on a footpath in Nelson in 1993. Kevin said to me, 'They got me in the right place with the first stab wound; it connected with my main artery. They knew where to hit.'

I relayed that to the cops and it turned out the first entry point of the weapon was into his back, but on a certain angle to locate a particular artery, which means the person who did it was trained in killing.

The case of Aaron Hopa was another extremely frustrating one. He and his English friend Robert Glazzard were both young men, 28 years old, working on a ship in the Persian Gulf as ROV [remotely operated vehicle] operators, surveying a Russian shipwreck.

They were working for Oceaneering International – Aaron had worked for them for six years – and they were on a ship called the *Seabulk Hercules*. But when the ship got back to Jebel Ali port in Dubai, Aaron and Robert were missing. Robert's body was found a week or so later, and Aaron's nearly two weeks after he went missing.

Aaron was from South Canterbury, and his parents Jim and Barbara, who approached *Sensing Murder* for help, still live in Geraldine. His Dad was a policeman who went to Dubai when his son was reported missing off the ship, and he didn't buy the theory that Aaron had just fallen off the ship – the ship had chest-high railings, so that was pretty hard to comprehend.

A pathologist in Dubai examined Aaron's body after it was recovered floating in the Persian Gulf and couldn't see any sign of injury so he ruled the death was accidental. But Jim Hopa got the Timaru coroner to do a proper forensic examination, and the New Zealand pathologist found that Aaron had died as a result of being garotted.

There were 30 people on that boat, and two of them didn't come back – so that leaves 28 people of whom one or two are murderers. We had some strong messages from Aaron on *Sensing Murder* that let us know who the murderers were. We have their names, we know roughly where we can find them but New Zealand's Police and Foreign Affairs have washed their hands of the case, each saying it's not their responsibility to investigate further.

I'm only speculating: is it because of politics? Is it because of the relationships between countries, imports and exports, that kind of thing? This is Dubai we're talking about here – Arabs, money, big shipping company. Aaron's Dad was a cop, worked for the government, and his own government won't allow him to go over and investigate. Yet it's his son we're talking about.

I believe it's one of the worst things you can experience, losing a child, especially in that fashion. Your own government that you work for won't let you follow it through and won't even put a team of people over there. I can't imagine the frustration and the heartache.

There are a lot of people out there who judge, ridicule and belittle what we do on *Sensing Murder*. Sometimes this can be because they don't have the experience in their own lives of seeing spirit, and sometimes it's because they refuse to allow other possibilities into their worldview. I believe they have the right to their point of view, but no one has the right to tell me I'm not seeing spirit.

If you want to take a crack at me, tell me why I'm seeing it then? They can't prove me wrong because I've been honest, loyal and true all the way along. I sometimes get quite fed up about it because there are a lot of vindictive people out there.

For instance, the morning after *Sensing Murder* won its second Qantas Media Award, in 2008, the *Truth* newspaper ran a picture of me on its front cover with a huge headline, 'Sensing Murder cursed'. They'd spoken to 'New Zealand's most well-known witch' who has nothing to do with *Sensing Murder*, and got her to say how we were all rubbish, fake and fraud. On and on the article went – bottom line is they knew that *Sensing Murder* would sell their paper, and that's why they put us on the front. A lot of the scepticism out there is very self-serving.

It might surprise people to hear that I'm sceptical too. I've learnt not to take spirit at face value. They have to prove themselves to me before I fully trust who they are and what they've got to say. That's important in any setting, and in a scenario like *Sensing Murder*, it's absolutely vital.

CHAPTER TWENTY-FOUR

Cooking up Soul Food

AS I WALK in the light of unconditional love, my life falls into place as it's meant to. I was extremely fortunate in 2005 to attract the attention of independent television producer Tracy Nodwell, who has a company called Showdown Productions.

Tracy had watched *Sensing Murder* when the first series came out and was fascinated by it. She's told me she thought the 'guy with the shaggy hair' was good talent, and late in 2006 she started putting together a TV programme idea that she called 'Soul Food'. Then she contacted me via my website, explaining she had a TV series idea to discuss.

I'd known a year before that I was to meet someone called Tracy, so when she said, 'Hi, my name's Tracy from Showdown', I just said, 'Oh, okay, I'll meet you.'

I was up north having a holiday but I drove all the way down to Auckland to meet with her. She didn't know that at the time – but I knew I had to meet her. We got on like a house on fire and I liked the programme idea (we finished editing the pilot for that very idea in November 2008).

In the months after our first meeting we hung out together a lot (she was trying to get her head around talking to dead people, and dead people talking back!), and became really good friends.

At that stage I was working really hard doing around six or seven readings a day, and I was often very drained at the end of each day. She tried to find me an agent, but because I wasn't an actor no one was interested. So she sat down and designed a 12-month calendar for me. She knew me well enough to know that I needed to have time in there for my son, who I have every second week, and that I need variety as I get bored quickly. She put in private readings, workshops, the live shows that we call 'Soul Food' and which we now take all around New Zealand, a tour of Australia, working tours to Samoa and Vanuatu (taking a group of 30 clients to each), and luncheons.

She took me out for lunch again, and this time hit me with the 12-month schedule, and the proposal that she become my agent. I was so relieved, moved and excited that I cried. We have been working as a team ever since, and she always keeps me motivated and focused. She has a fantastic team around her at Showdown Talent, and I just feel like a member of the family. I would not have been able to help so many people learn and understand the spirit world without the support and knowledge of those who work on our team.

That was back in January 2007. We have gone from strength to strength since then, and she has helped me cope with some of the demands that have arisen from my appearances on *Sensing Murder*. For instance, when the programme's on air, I get around 200 emails a day, and that is impossible for one person to deal with appropriately. It's been challenging to meet everyone's needs, but our goal was and still is to help as many people as possible. Money from one show helps us get to the next and so on.

I believe I have achieved so much because I've given so much. My reward comes in seeing somebody's pain lift off, in knowing that their little one's right beside them. That's the reward.

Soul Food has built up to the point where I do several shows a week around New Zealand and Australia. The audiences can vary in size from about 60, right up to 1400.

CHAPTER 25

'I'm just the railway conductor'

ONE EVENING I was due to do a show in the Capitaine Bougainville Theatre in Whangarei, New Zealand's northernmost city. It's a great theatre, and yet when I walked in that afternoon I was immediately overwhelmed by spirit presences. 'Whoa, I don't like it here.' I knew I had work to do.

Since my experience at the Milford Spiritualist Church I've never forgotten how important it is to prepare for the shows properly – to clear the room of negative energies and be respectful.

This time, the feelings were so extreme, I couldn't talk to any of the stage crew, couldn't even talk to Tracy, nothing. I just immediately closed my eyes and began praying. I prayed and prayed, acknowledging the presence of spirits, asking for a clearance, asking anyone who was lost whether I was allowed to work there. I asked if they wanted to cross through because I could show them how to. The next thing I knew there were people coming out of the woodwork, spiritually, and I asked for the white light to be open to allow them to cross through if that's what they wanted to do. I gave them plenty of time and when we came back to the theatre a bit later on it felt really good and we went on and did a really amazing show.

Later, I got talking to a guy who has worked in the theatre for 10 years.

'When you first arrived here, how did you feel?' he asked.

I told him how it had been really weird. 'I felt really overwhelmed by lots of male spiritual energy in here, and I had to show them how to get through.'

He said, 'Oh that's really freaky! But it doesn't surprise me one little bit.'

'Why?' I asked, and he explained the background to the theatre building.

In 1975 there had been a fire on board a cargo vessel called *Capitaine Bougainville*. Sixteen of the crew and passengers of the cargo vessel died and the skipper was forced to abandon ship in mountainous seas off the coast of Whananaki, north of Whangarei. It was Northland's worst maritime disaster.

Northland Harbour Board tugs salvaged the vessel, and out of the salvage money came a substantial donation to the building of the theatre – hence the name, the Capitaine Bougainville Theatre – and the ship's bell, oars and flotation are displayed outside.

There are many stories of people having strange experiences in the theatre, and people who work in the city council there talk openly about the theatre's ghosts and spirits. Many say that it feels weird, or as if people are watching them as they walk up the back corridor. A lot of Maori productions will not use the venue until a karakia has been said for them.

Then he went on to say that another psychic had been there and had been unable to read. You must ask permission if you can be there or not. It's so important that your ego doesn't lead you to forget your discipline.

I always ask if I'm allowed to be in the theatre. There was one theatre I went to that had an old projectionist's booth, and this old man was standing in it, high above the seating. He gave me a wave.

'Who's that guy up there?' I asked, waving back at him.

'What fella?' the manager asked.

'The guy up there who's in the window waving at me. The projectionist.'

'Oh, no the projectionist had a heart attack eight years ago,' the manager told me. 'He'd worked here all his life.'

'So you're saying I'm seeing a dead person and he's waving at me?' It was true: he'd had a heart attack a few years earlier in his projectionist's booth, but to me he was still there. I then therefore said to the projectionist: 'Hi mate, how you going, do you mind if I read tonight?'

'Nah,' he said. 'It'd be really good. Something different.'

Out of respect I had gained his permission to be there, and so the night went smoothly. As soon as you stop doing that you can get into trouble. It's similar to not removing your shoes at someone's house, even if it was a rule of the house. It's showing disrespect. It's the same thing but on a bigger scale, that's all.

Whenever I do anything spiritually – and that includes shows and private readings – I prepare with prayer, and I always burn a candle to bring in light energy and add a nice tone to the room, and for some reason, it makes me feel safe. When I was little, I'd never sleep without the light on, so it's the same sort of feeling. Then, when I've finished the show, I blow the candle out. I also have a ritual where at the beginning of a show or a reading, I take off my bracelet as a sign to myself that it's time to start work. Little things like that all help me to get started, and help smooth the way into 'the zone' that I need to be in to bring spirit forward for the audience.

When you consider that everyone in the audience is bringing spirits, that's a big crowd in my head. If there are 1000 people in the audience, and they all have at least two people with them who are dead, that's 3000 souls I'm looking at. It's very busy: the spirits are all around, trying to come forward, and I see them as little orbs of light but when I focus on them with my third eye they come closer and I start to see and hear what they're telling me.

I'll ask spirit, 'Where am I supposed to go?' and I'll hear 'Over here, over here, over here, over here!'

'Okay, one at a time, folks!' That's what I actually say. 'Just one at a time would be good, just slow down and we'll get it going.' To me it becomes like a railway station and I'm just the railway conductor trying to organise them so we can get a nice smooth ride.

Let's say a spirit person has ridden his motorbike through the front of the stage. Now, that will get my attention, so I'll say, 'Hey mate, nice bike, park it up so we can chat.'

He does, and it's a Ducati bike – very nice – and of course he's boasting about it.

'What's your name?' I ask.

'Hey, it's Dave.'

'Hi, Dave, who are you trying to find?'

'My sister.'

'Okay, where is she?'

'Over there.'

I ask him to go stand next to her and I watch where he goes and when he stops he says, 'That's her just here.'

'Cheers, Dave, just hold on a minute.'

I then ask for a microphone to be delivered and I say to the woman in the audience, 'I have a bloke called Dave standing next to you. He says he's your brother and he's showing off on his Ducati bike. I feel he passed on his bike and clearly did not have a chance to say goodbye.'

And the woman with her mouth open wide and tears running down her face says, 'Yes, that's my brother!'

I then ask the spirit to come back on stage and tell me more if he would like to, and the read begins. That's how we locate each other.

Out of 1000 in the audience, what are the odds of getting that? Truly awesome!

Sometimes it takes time to sort out who belongs to who.

I remember one show where I was drawn to work with a woman sitting in one of the back rows who was not coping with the loss of her husband.

He was finding it very difficult to come back and connect – he wanted to but he didn't know how to start off, but her need for healing was great. There were a lot of spirit people around her and I had to work quite hard to be clear about who was there for her. One spirit near her jumped in straight away and was trying to get my attention, and I instantly identified him as 'Christopher', and the fact that he had died by hanging. The man sitting next to the woman said, 'Oh, he's mine!' – Christopher was one of his spirits, and so I knew he had nothing to do with the woman I was trying to work with. But I knew I had to set Christopher aside and just stick with the lady.

Another point that came out of that particular reading is that I need to be very respectful of where the living person is at in their life. This lady was grieving so bad she wanted to end her life to be with her husband – that's what I was seeing, but I didn't say that publicly as I didn't want to embarrass her. Part of her healing was to understand that her husband was okay, and that he was still there for her.

One of the images the spirit kept insisting on was a police-type picture, and for a while that didn't seem to make any sense. But she went away at half time and had a think about that and realised he was referring to the band Police, who they had especially loved and had seen in concert together. By the end of her reading she looked quite different, refreshed, as if she had had a cleansing shower, and

193

she told me she believed her life could now go on. I think it's pretty special.

It can be very hard to understand the symbolism of an individual read – spirit language is a different language to our daily language, but it all comes out in the wash if you have patience.

Spirit is in another dimension which means it's hard for me to talk to them and I get frustrated, as a bloke, because I want the answers now just like everybody else. But we know it doesn't happen that way. The language of the spirits is unique. You never know what you're going to get.

The goal for me in a show is to communicate with people in spirit. Clearly, that's the ultimate. I don't know who the people are who come to my shows. I don't sit people in the audience – and neither does my agent. What's the point of cheating? I don't even contemplate doing that. My son would not look up to me the way that he does now. Why would I want to be disloyal to him?

People come of their own accord and they sit where they want. I don't know who they are and I just ask, if somebody wants to come through, come through. If I don't get something I just don't get it and I'm not going to make up anything. One night, I was talking to a young woman who was sitting in the front row, and I said to her, 'You had a pet duck as a child, eh?'

She probably thought that was a bit strange, but she said she had.

'Oh cool,' I said, 'because it's just here.'

Everybody was laughing and I said, 'That's okay, you can laugh, but I do see pet ducks too.'

Then a girl in the very same row, about 15 people across maybe, put her hand up and said, 'But I had a pet duck too as a child.' Everyone cracked up, and I was thinking, 'How am I going to get around this?' She wanted a message too, you see, and she thought that as she'd had a pet duck as well, perhaps the message was for her.

Just then, an old lady in spirit appeared by the first girl and said,

'You just tell that girl down the end that her pet duck died of natural causes and my girl's pet duck died because her Daddy put it in the pot.'

So I spoke it, and it brought the house down. It was the most hilarious thing you could say as a medium, and the girl at the end said 'Yeah, my duck died of natural causes,' and the first girl said, 'Yeah, my Daddy cooked my duck.'

It was very funny in one way, but the girl was really upset, and her partner was consoling her. Then I said, 'It was your grandmother, your Mum's mother, who just came through and told me that.' So I was yakking away to the grandmother.

Meanwhile, there was a big wall of curtains down the side of the theatre and there was a man in spirit standing behind the curtains, but ducking his head around them, out and back, as if he was too shy to come out.

'Hey, mate?' I said to him. 'Come over here.'

'Nah,' he said.

I turned back to the girl, and I said, 'Your grandmother's bringing her husband in, they're together which is really neat, but the interesting thing is that now I've got a bloke trying to get my attention but he's behind the curtain over there. He's related to you but he's a little bit nervous.'

I looked back across to where he was standing, and he was half out of the curtain, pounding his chest and saying, 'Dad.'

'I'm kind of thinking your Dad's passed of a heart attack and you didn't get a chance to say goodbye to him. But he wants you to know that he's okay but he's really unsure about this situation.'

Well, she fell to pieces. She'd just lost her Dad. So we started reading with him and I said, 'Come out and talk to me', and he started telling me little bits and pieces and he apologised for the duck and then she started to get the giggles, which was good because she was crying and laughing at the same time.

195

But there's even more to this story. I looked at the Dad again and now he had a boy standing beside him, and then I started to cry because I knew I was going to have to talk about her brother.

'I've got some other stuff for you,' I told her. 'I've got this young boy, apparently he's your brother and he was killed in an accident, and he's with your Dad.'

Well, she lost it, her partner lost it, we all lost it, 200 people were crying because the duck brought the grandmother, who brought the grandfather, who brought the dad, who brought the little brother in. Her little brother was killed in a tractor accident on the farm and her Dad wanted them to know that they were together and that they were happy.

When we come to a story like this, which is admittedly both funny and sad, it comes down to a duck quacking to get my attention and ultimately bringing all these people in to let me know that her little brother had passed by accident on a tractor on the farm, and he was with her Dad. That's phenomenal.

I think that every single person who has a reading, in some way, shape or form, will in their own way come to a conclusion about understanding faith.

It can be very frustrating when I'm bringing in information from spirit and it doesn't seem to be making sense. I'm trying to find the owner but nothing seems to fit. I really need those little pieces of confirmation so that, as a medium, I know I'm in the right space, because there's nothing worse than getting an email the next day saying 'Well, you were talking to that lady but I was sitting just behind her and everything you said fitted *me*.'

I ask 'Why didn't you put your hand up?'

'Oh, I was too scared.' So those situations are really difficult, but you just have to go to work and try and battle through. Trying to find the person belonging to the spirit is damn hard.

Spirits can be shy themselves, especially the spirits of children. At one Soul Food show in our most southern city, Invercargill, there was a woman in the audience who had a blanket around her. I asked her, 'Do you want to ask me something?'

'Yeah,' she said. 'Is my little girl all right?'

'More than likely,' I said, but at that moment I didn't have the spirit coming through.

The woman asked: 'How come the children don't come through as much as the adults?'

I laughed. 'Can you imagine what it would be like for a little kid at an adult's party to try and push their way to the front to grab the chippies off the table? It's very difficult for them to push through.'

This is the case, even though the child's spirit is ageless and timeless, because the manifestation to me is how they were in this life. So I said, 'I'll just step everyone out, hang on a minute.'

I said to spirit, 'Everyone else step away and let this child come through.'

Then I said, 'It's really weird. I've got one child over there laughing at me, and I've got another little girl tap-dancing right beside me and they're coming through together and there's another one with a big R and I don't understand.'

It turned out that the lady I was talking to, and the lady sitting next to her, were connected and had both lost girls. The first lady had also lost her niece, who was a Down Syndrome girl whose name started with R. They had thought the girls would all be together, and now they were greatly comforted to know that was the case.

At the end of the day, no one will understand that message but them. That's it. It's not about anybody else, it's about the person I'm getting it for. It's not about me proving to you, it's about understanding it.

Other times, spirit comes through with a message that seems to make no sense to the person it's supposedly for.

We were at a show in Auckland and there was a couple in the

audience and I had already established a link for the woman with her son, who had passed over.

We'd already talked for a while when I said, 'Oh, it's really weird, he's telling me to tell you to look under the bed. This is for you and your boyfriend: you've got to look under your bed when you get home tonight.'

Of course everyone started laughing and thinking, what's under the bed? And they were saying, 'Yeah okay, that's kind of weird but, whatever, fine thanks.'

And then the guy, her partner, said, 'The bed's only a few centimetres off the ground.' Everyone laughed. It didn't seem to make any sense.

'Even so, look under the bed,' I said. 'Save an argument.'

Well, they sent me an email explaining what happened. On the way to the show that night they'd got into one of those stupid fights that couples have, where she'd lost her lip gloss and she blamed him for it. He said he'd never touched it, etc. When they got home that night, after the show, they lifted up the bed and there was the lip gloss!

Once I've made the connection between the spirit and the person sitting in the audience, there are two things going on for me. One is to do with thoughts – the headspace of the person in the audience. Thought waves are like radio waves, you can't see them but you can tune into them with the guidance of spirit. So, the goal is to recognise, what's happening with this person? Oh well, she's got lots going on, she's just too busy, she needs a good holiday, she's depressed, she's this, she's that. Okay, anyone can do that to a certain extent, by reading your clothes, looking into your eyes, seeing your aura, seeing what's going on.

But then there's the person's spirit family, and you can tune into that vibration or that radio frequency at the same time. You need to focus your energy into that different frequency.

The easiest way to explain it to you is by using radio stations as

198

an example. The Rock and The Breeze are two very different radio stations, with very different vibrational tones. One is loud and grungy, one is really mellow and fun – they're skewed differently, and run along different lines or layers. Thought and spirit are comparable to that.

Every time I go on stage it's different – you never know what you're going to get and it all depends on the crowd and their expectations, and it can depend on where I'm at too.

If I'm stressed or ill, I have to put my own personal issues completely to the side and try and do the best I can. But once I've clicked into 'the zone' I stop worrying and I just get on with it. It's perfect focus, nice and smooth.

To get into 'the zone' I have to be relaxed and if the audience are all uptight and nervous then that's when a bit of humour comes into it to make them laugh and relax. It's not a forced humour, but I've just realised that if you tell a few yarns to make everyone relax, it stops them focusing on their expectations. And when they're not thinking about who's coming through it'll just happen. If they're focusing on wanting their Mum to come through, then it's more than likely that she won't come through at all.

Some people *expect* their person who's passed over to come through. But that person on the other side might not be ready for that. It may not be an appropriate time to discuss personal details in front of an audience; it may be that the person was very private or it may be that someone else in the audience needs a message more. There are many reasons why someone might not come through in that setting.

There are a lot of factors that contribute to the message getting through. But I've always believed that whoever is meant to get it, will eventually get it. It might not happen then and there, but somewhere down the line, it will all make sense. You just have to leave your expectations at the door.

CHAPTER TWENTY-SIX

Walking in light

DURING this incredible journey that I'm on in this life, I believe I'm here to learn and experience as much as I can in a fun, positive way. I will relish the sun when it visits; I will play in the rain; I will be a dad, a mate to all and I will live every moment as if it were my last. I truly believe life's what we make it. I reckon we should go with the flow, trusting each day as it comes along.

We are only here once in this body so we should make the most of it – but I absolutely believe that we can come back for more experiences, good or bad, if we need to for our spiritual learning.

At the moment I am just content to keep helping people. As for my future, I trust what the creator and spirit have lined up for me. I trust them, and will trust their guidance as new life experiences come to hand. One day at a time – keeping it real – is so important to me. I believe that before coming back to this earthly experience I sat with the creator and had a conversation about what to do while here to grow and to learn.

And so I have faith knowing that I have chosen well. We have to try to be the best we can, even though we all falter at times; we will all stumble from time to time. Guilty! We are only human, after all, but we aim for the stars and so we keep trying.

Life itself comes down to experiences. Your job is to learn to understand who you are. Understanding brings release. We are here to remember where we have been, and to complete the jigsaw of life. I had a big piece of my life puzzle missing until I truly gave myself to the creator, angels and spirit people. Now I feel complete.

There are lots of different factors in how you look at your life. I just personally think we need to get off the sofa! Get off it and get out there – live your dream. We cannot control anything but ourselves so why sweat the stuff we can't control.

I am blessed by my gift, but I really want people to understand that everyone can learn to see and feel spirit, and to have that blessing in their lives. We lose our feeling for spirit because we are distracted by our daily lives, and the busyness of this world.

All these things make us ignorant of what's really going on in our own lives. When we're pretending that everything's okay and we're distracting ourselves with being busy and with the fantasy world of our television sets, we're really being blind to our own selves.

When we get to the point of trying to shut off from these things, by creating quiet moments of meditation in our lives, we begin to make steps forward in our relationship with spirit. It comes down to realising that if your intuition is strong it can be stronger.

This is a massive realisation for people. There are many, many people out there who have had something happen to them – a strong spiritual experience of some kind. For instance, it might have been that when their dad died, you know, dad sat on the end of their bed. Most normal people will tell you that they have had one experience like this, if not more.

I have those every day. I'm lucky as. But by the same token, there's balance to that and I have to switch off, otherwise I'd just go over the edge.

I love my life. I live near the sea and I am lucky enough to have a boat that I take out into the Waitemata Harbour for fishing trips with my son. On the boat, no one's allowed to talk about dead people, although they do all come fishing with me.

My home is a no-go zone for spirits, too, except for members of my own family. The others all have to wait. This was something I had to learn, as I've explained elsewhere in this book.

I feel extremely blessed to have this gift, to walk in the light of unconditional love, and to dedicate myself to helping people in need. With the support of the creator, and my guardian angels and spirit guides, I see miracles every day – lives that were halted by unbearable grief are able to move on with a new understanding of life and spirituality. I love my work, because to see someone's pain lift off them, not from me but from the messages they receive from spirit, well, it's just unreal. It's like a miracle unfolding. It's primo.

I have seen too many miracles to not be certain about what I'm doing.

Beliefs are beliefs. We can all believe whatever we want. But if you want to live in the light and be loved it's up to you and the door's open.

To walk in light is to be at peace with everything in life, to accept that everything happens for a reason even if we can't at first understand what that reason is. To walk in light is to accept who you are, and to be honest and true.

I believe the white light is my saviour and I will honour the light until I cross into the light …

Until I return home.

FREQUENTLY ASKED QUESTIONS

People always have a lot of questions about the nature of the spirit world and the work I do as a psychic medium. The following are some of the most common questions I get asked at all my shows, events and readings.

1. What are your thoughts on reincarnation?

I believe in reincarnation and past lives although it is ultimately up to each one of us to decide for ourselves. Let's say that your dad has passed over and the family believes he has been reincarnated through grandson Johnny. When you go for a reading do you still speak with your dad? My thought is that the creator would always reflect your dad in hologram form as the creator takes a blueprint of each of his/her children. This, of course, always brings hope and love as the creator would never leave you lonely.

2. **When children pass in to spirit, do they continue to grow older?**

   This all depends on the spirit's journey of choice. For example, if a baby passes over, in some cases the spirit child may choose to stay the same because the family will only ever have the baby in their minds and hearts. In other cases the child will continue to grow, just as the parents see the child growing in their own minds. On *Sensing Murder* I recall Amber Lee Cruickshank came through in spirit as a 17-year-old: she said a few things and then changed into a two-and-a-half-year-old. I remember saying, 'I've got someone's little angel here,' then the reading began. I later met Amber Lee's mother and on the day of that reading she would have been 17 years old. Her mum believed she was alive all those years and saw her in her mind's eye growing older. Sadly, as we know, Amber Lee will never return home as she has crossed over. She proved this to her mum on the day of her seventeenth birthday. So it all depends on the journey that each spirit chooses.

3. **What can I do to help my children with their spirituality and encourage their gifts?**

   Praise them, support them, but never force them to see and do things. They are naturally gifted and if it is meant to be the gift will continue. Our kids see a lot of positive and negative things. Always tell them the angels will guide and protect them and that they will always be safe. Support them with love. Children will always see both positive and negative spirits. This can be frightening for them. Reassure them the angels will always be there to guide and protect them. They will always be safe – no matter how scared they are – with the angels beside them.

4. **When someone passes from suicide, do they cross over into the spirit world or do they remain 'in limbo'?**

As with reincarnation, this could be a whole chapter of a book! Again, it depends on the situation or circumstances surrounding the suicide. I believe if you take your life 'clear of mind' or in other words if drugs and alcohol are not involved then you will cross over as they will be waiting for you. However, if you commit suicide under the influence of drugs or medications (anti-depressants, etc.) then it is possible you will not cross over and will find yourself in limbo or lost until you can learn to understand what you are about. You will have to wait there until you see the light of self-love. Often those who cross in this way are very difficult to talk to in spirit. However, we can help them cross by praying for them and by their extended spirit family reaching out to help them.

5. **How do we identify and deal with a presence in the house which is causing discomfort?**

Lots of things can be done in this situation to clear a presence from the house. The best thing is to contact a local medium, or spiritual group, and get them to bless the house. Stay positive, light candles, and call on the angels for support.

6. **What are orbs and can you explain the meaning of orbs in photos?**

   It has only been possible to catch the spirits as orbs with the development of the digital camera – before that the shutter speed was just too slow. The orbs appear as circles as a way of spirits saying they are close to us.

7. **Can Kelvin solve mysteries like the disappearance of Madeleine McCann?**

   I will only do so if I am asked by the family concerned. In all cases I believe it is disrespectful for me to investigate a case unless I have their permission. There is also no point without permission as any information will fall on deaf ears.

8. **I see spirit often, and I'm wondering how you control it? Is there an off switch?**

   Meditate, and designate a special time of the day to talk to the spirits. This way your mind, body and soul will attune with them and you will become a team. Ask to receive messages to understand them and yourself; ask what it is they would like to share with you. After you give thanks, ask to be closed until your next special time with spirit. This will help you sleep better too!

9. **Can you please explain to me your thoughts on God?**

   My God is all accepting, all understanding and most importantly, all loving. The creator for me is everywhere: everywhere I see and everywhere I am.